WHO I
ALWAYS WAS

WHO I ALWAYS WAS

— *A Memoir* —

THERESA OKOKON

ATRIA BOOKS

New York   Amsterdam/Antwerp   London   Toronto   Sydney   New Delhi

An Imprint of Simon & Schuster, LLC
1230 Avenue of the Americas
New York, NY 10020

Interior photograph credits: pp. ii, 27, 183, and 264: courtesy of Theresa Okokon;
p. 91: Vanessa Simonet; p. 265: Dan Marie Ajala

"Me Llamo Theresa" first appeared (in similar form) in *Hippocampus Magazine*.

Some names and identifying characteristics have been changed.

First Atria Books hardcover edition February 2025

ATRIA BOOKS and colophon are trademarks of Simon & Schuster, LLC

For information about special discounts for bulk purchases, please contact Simon &
Schuster Special Sales at 1-866-506-1949 or business@simonandschuster.com.

The Simon & Schuster Speakers Bureau can bring authors to your live event. For
more information or to book an event, contact the Simon & Schuster Speakers
Bureau at 1-866-248-3049 or visit our website at www.simonspeakers.com.

Interior design by Jill Putorti

Manufactured in the United States of America

1 3 5 7 9 10 8 6 4 2

Library of Congress Cataloging-in-Publication Data is available upon request.

ISBN 978-1-6680-0895-9
ISBN 978-1-6680-0897-3 (ebook)

for Uncle Ato
who was committed to me knowing my story

and for Minnie
who gave me someone to keep alive

I just got one more thing to tell you: 'cuz words are vitamins, and life is short.

—ANI DIFRANCO

CONTENTS

CONTENTS

Part Three

• • •

MOTHER'S NOTE

It is no secret to my mom, my siblings, or my mom's side of the family that I've set out to write this book. Many of the stories held in these pages are ones that I have heard and reheard them tell. These are the stories I've told and retold myself, for as long as I could speak (including, as you will learn, the story of what my actual first word was, anyhow).

On the other hand, many of these stories are ones I am learning now, for the first time. Many of the characters and versions of the truth presented here are things my family does not talk about, words I have never heard my mother utter aloud. And it would be foolish of me to presume the silence has been accidental, much less unintentional.

As long as you're telling the truth, my mom once told me, *I'm fine with it.* I had just completed a draft of an essay held in these pages, and I had called my mom to check in on her. I was beginning to question, as I would many times throughout the course of composing this manuscript, if my voice mattered, if it was worthy of being heard. I was doubting whether or not I had the right to tell a story that did not only belong to me. *What do you mean, "the truth"?* I asked her, my voice trailing, my mind drifting.

Because the thing about real life is that it has no singular nor easy narrative. As a storyteller and a writer, I fully recognize that—in many ways—we are all just characters in each other's stories. And the meaning of the plot, the truth of it, varies depending on our perspectives. My mother is neither a writer nor even much of a storyteller unless one of us kids cajoles her into it—but lucky for me, she is a person who knows that the only truth in life is that there is no capital *T* truth.

Some people feel like you aren't supposed to say things, I heard my mom respond across the phone line. *Like, out of respect for the family, you shouldn't air out anyone's dirty laundry. But not me, I'm not like that. I don't care what people think. I wouldn't answer all of your questions if I didn't want you to know. I wouldn't tell you if I didn't want you to tell anyone else, because I know you will.*

Someone should tell it.

PROLOGUE
BORROWED CONTEXT

G hana (pronounced GAH-nahhh, and officially named the Republic of Ghana) is a West African country sandwiched between Côte d'Ivoire and Togo, with the Atlantic Ocean to the south and Burkina Faso to the north. The capital city of Accra boasts a population of about 2.6 million people, comparable to Chicago.[1] Ghana is home[2] to savannahs, rainforests, and the second largest number of people in all of West Africa. As I was researching for this essay collection, I found my Google search results for Ghana easily skewed[3] in a positive direction—with the top result for "how is Ghana perceived" pointing to the way Ghana is respected for the long-standing stability of its postcolonial government.

1. I was born in Chicago but raised in Wisconsin—where I lived until I was twenty-four years old. I have three siblings: a big sister, who is two years older than me; a little sister, who is just under two years younger than me; and a little brother, who is six years younger than me. Only my little sister and I were born in the same place, because my family was moving around as my dad sought out a tenure-track, university faculty position. Despite my birthplace, Wisconsin is and always has been home for me.

2. When I was growing up, my mom would sometimes refer to "home" with an implied capital *H*, and when she did: she meant Ghana—where she was born and raised. My mom grew up in Winneba, a small coastal town about an hour outside of Accra, and she is one of my grandfather's twelve children. His first wife, the mother of my uncle Ato—the sibling my mom has the closest relationship with—died, and my grandfather then remarried my grandmother. My mom is number six of her mom's children, and number nine of her siblings overall.

3. I'm not sure I have ever heard a negative stereotype about Ghana. Have you? That's the thing about Google, though: What it tells you is determined by what you already believe. So even if I wanted a different perspective, so long as Google knows it is me at the keyboard, the story I'm told will very likely be the story I've always been told. Unless I find a new way to ask the question.

More on that later...

In 2019, the Ghana Tourism Authority (GTA) launched a campaign called "The Year of Return," in an effort to make Ghana the destination for Black Americans seeking a home base in response to the diaspora caused by the transatlantic slave trade.[4] In a *Washington Post* article, the GTA's chief executive said, "We want to remind our kin over there that there is a place you can escape to. That is Africa." The first time I read this article, the word "kin" leapt off my computer screen and into my lap. To me: Ghana is family, and it wants to be that—for everyone. In fact, this invitation from the GTA is nothing new: for decades Ghana has been a leader in the Pan-African movement, and the country's flag is a demonstration of that.

In 1821, Ghana was colonized by the British, who referred to the country as the "Gold Coast" because of its huge supply of and market for gold. More than one hundred years later, on March 6, 1957—when my mother was five years old—Ghana and three other colonies were the first to achieve independence from the Crown.[5]

---

4. My family is not in America because of the slave trade; rather: We chose to be here. My mom's elder siblings, including Uncle Ato, immigrated in the late 1950s and early '60s, and my mom eventually followed as a teenager in 1969. My grandfather had run out of money to continue to send her to school, and Uncle Ato—who was living in Wisconsin and building a life as a Pan-African community organizer in Milwaukee—sponsored her. While helping Uncle Ato raise his children, my mom enrolled in night school, completed her GED, and got into Marquette University for undergrad. While there, she would visit the library and exchange smiles with a handsome, round-faced, Nigerian man with big white teeth. Years later, that man would become my father.

5. My brother tells me that on recent visits with Uncle Ato—who moved back home to Ghana when I was a teenager—our uncle referred to the British as "our colonial overlords." But I never heard him speaking that way when we were growing up—not my parents either. In my 1980s and 1990s Wisconsin home, racism was never discussed. And the fact that colonialism is rooted in racism is not something I would understand until I am an adult, educating myself on the internet.

Under its newfound independence from our colonial over-lords, Ghana developed a national flag, depicted by horizontal stripes of red, gold, and green, with a black star in the middle. The flag was designed by Theodosia Okoh, a well-respected artist. She wanted the red to stand for the blood of the ancestors who had struggled for this independence. The green represents Ghana's natural agricultural wealth, and the gold symbolizes the country's mineral resources—literal gold. But there is dispute over whose decision it was to include the flag's centerpiece: a black star that has come to represent the Pan-African struggle for freedom.

- Story version one: Ghana's first president added the black star as an acknowledgment of his friend Marcus Garvey's Black Star Line, a shipping program meant to transport Africans back to Africa.
- Story version two: Theodosia has said that *she* included the star to show that Black is beautiful and something worth striving to be.
- What is not disputed: No one ever told Theodosia that her flag design was selected as the winner. Instead, she found out with everyone else in the coun-

try, when her unaccredited, winning design was announced in the newspapers.

If you went to Google today, I cannot promise which story you'd find. This might be because the algorithm is attempting to reinforce what it thinks you already believe; or it might be because some facts are just fickle. Shifty. Ever-changing and near impossible to validate.

In my suburban American education, I learned that Betsy Ross designed the American flag, and that is a fact I would never think to question. I'd never think to open any internet tabs to verify the story, and I'd bet money that most kids of my generation would be able to parrot this fact to you without much thought. Betsy Ross is an American household name, yet I cannot recall anyone in my extended Ghanaian family ever uttering Theodosia[6] Okoh's name.

My mom would never fly an American flag[7] from a pole in our front yard, but to this day, she keeps a small American flag in the same vase as a small Ghanaian flag centered on top of her piano—which, fun fact, she doesn't know how to play. My mother bought the piano so that my siblings and I would learn how to play it, and I imagine she's kept it because in some way, having a piano in her home is simply part of the identity she has developed for herself. I don't think my mother plans to move back Home to Ghana like Uncle Ato has done, or as Marcus Garvey may have wanted, and she doesn't need to. She doesn't need to play to feel a connection to her piano, and she doesn't need to return to Ghana to feel a connection to her Home.

---

6. Theodosia has her own Wikipedia page. Her husband—the Head of Civil Service for Ghana's first president—does not. I love this fact. I came up in the Spice Girls era of Girl Power; and Destiny's Child told me that I should strive to buy my own car and my own house, and Beyoncé declared that she, I, and Theodosia run this mutha. I am drawn like a moth to the flame of this factoid about Theodosia and her lesser-wiki'd husband. The flag we're flyin'? She designed it.

7. Most readers of this essay collection will know that the colors of the American flag are red, white, and blue. And yet there are earlier versions of this essay wherein I state that fact plainly, as if it needed to be demonstrated, taught, or proven to anyone.

Earlier versions of this essay included a story about this one time when my mom rejected a full-size, free American flag with a purchase at a Kohl's department store while taking me shopping for new school clothes. It included a story about this one time when I was driving in Vermont and these two White kids in a black pickup truck drove past me on a scary and snowy road—their torsos hung from the windows, their middle fingers rigid, their lungs screaming at me to go back home, and their American flag flapping in the wind as I caught my breath. It included a story about this one time when I was in Maine and I convinced myself that every truck in town had a giant Confederate flag on it, until I finally realized it was just one guy who I kept seeing—and that just one was enough. These stories took up several pages and they existed in an effort to prove to you that racism is real, present, and current. They existed because, contrary to my Ghanaian ancestors who spilled blood because they knew their independence was necessary, I have spilled unnecessary ink—for you—because I believed I

9

had to. I am not proud of this. This tendency to prove myself, to provide evidence of my experience, to convince and attempt to teach "you" is directly connected to the fact that I am a Black woman who grew up as a Black girl in almost entirely White environments. I want to be a Black writer whose imagined "you" are Black and brown people. I make an effort to be that writer. But the simple and uncomfortable fact of my existence is that "you" have almost always been White people. And *I* have almost always been drowning in the act of performing myself for you.

I hope that I have successfully edited out all incidences of my attempts to combat the skepticism of an imagined "you" from every page and drop of ink on these pages. I know that I have failed, and I am not proud of this.

Anyhow, black star and GTA invitations notwithstanding, the Pan-African movement is about much more than Ghana alone. So is this book.[8] Because only half of my blood and half of the branches of my family tree come from there.

---

8. Research for the essays contained in this collection involved interviewing teachers, friends, and family members. It involved eating the mentioned foods, listening to old music, watching old TV shows, and looking at old Zillow listings. I dug through photo albums, reread papers I wrote dating back to eighth grade, and opened dozens and dozens of internet tabs. And yet there are still things I will never know. There are still pieces of my narrative that continue to shift and change. Take the multiversion origin story of Ghana's black star, for example.

I remember reading that the Ghanaian government chose Theodosia Okoh's tricolored-stripe flag design, and then added the black star to the center as a symbol of unity among all Black people. I am certain I read this fact because I distinctly recall making note of it and then struggling to devise a metaphor around it.

Pan-Africanism is about unity and kinship—which reminds me of my mom's family, the Yarneys: Because the Yarneys (like Ghana, and herein lies the easy part of the metaphor) embrace anyone who is connected to the family—by blood, by marriage, or by choice. Like me, my mom has a dozen aunts and uncles, making her half of my family tree wide and deeply rooted. I don't have to meet every Yarney to feel a connection to them.

There is a Yarney Facebook group where the moderator makes daily posts to wish happy birthday to all the Yarneys born on that day, and my big sister's husband gets a birthday shout-out just like everyone else. During the early days of the pandemic, one of my cousins began hosting Yarney family Zooms, and Yarneys from all over the world—in the United States, Ghana, and parts of Europe—would pop up on my computer screen like a Black *Brady Bunch*. Every time someone new joined, we would trace back which uncle or auntie they descended from, and then wrap them into the fold: heart and celebration emojis coupled with giggles of hello from the elders who never caught on to the concept of mute-when-not-speaking. We Yarneys are like a familial GTA.

Everybody is kin, and once you're in—you're in. What a tidy, pretty little metaphor.

However, the story I remember reading indicated that the black star was added without communication or consent. Which . . . feels like the makings of a far less tidy, far less pretty little metaphor.

In the time between my first reading of this fact and when I went back to verify the detail: It disappeared. I read and reread all the wiki pages I could recall previously visiting. I googled and re-googled Theodosia—but couldn't find any mention of the Ghanaian government adding the star to her original design, with or without telling her first.

Ghana black star origins?

Theodosia Okoh, Ghana, consent?

Did anyone ask Theodosia if she wanted her flag to represent Pan-Africanism?

It was like I couldn't find the right words to ask my question and get the answer I was seeking. This time, Google insisted the star was all Theodosia's idea. Part of me worried that if I included the nonconsent detail, I'd be called out by fact-checkers—experts who knew more

13

about my mother's Home than I ever could. Every American knows Betsy Ross designed the flag; so am I even Ghanaian if I don't know the history of the black star? Would my Blackness be called into question? Would I be exposed as a fraud?

Like so many facts, my memory is also fickle. Shifty. And sometimes, I worry that I cannot even believe the story I am telling myself.

Fuck it, I finally told myself, my memory is evidence enough—isn't it?

This tendency to question the validity of my own memory—to seek evidence of my lived experiences—is directly connected to the fact that I have lived a life filled with shifting details. I have learned that what I have been told, believe, or remember is often not *not* the truth, but it is rarely the full truth either.

The last time I googled for details of Theodosia's flag, there were new stories about how Ghana today likes to tout the feminist narrative of having a flag designed by a woman, but that historically: girl power is not part of the story Ghana told about itself. As I read this, it felt like Google had finally caught up with the story I (the Spice Girls, Destiny's Child, and Beyoncé) had been seeking all along.

Fuck it, I told myself once again. *It's all going in.* What I remember, what I want to believe, what I was told, what I can verify now. It's all part of the story I'm going to tell.

•   •   •

Nigeria[9] (pronounced niyh-GEER-eee-uhhh, and officially the Federal Republic of Nigeria) is a West African country and the sixth most populated country in the world.[10] At just about 15 million people, Lagos (the capital city during my father's childhood) is among the globe's top twenty metropolitan areas, unlike any city in Wisconsin or Massachusetts (which I now claim[11] as home).

---

9. My dad was born and raised in Nigeria. When he spoke of "home" with an implied capital *H*, he meant Nigeria. But other than knowing the name of his home country, I cannot recall my dad ever saying much of anything about where he was from.

10. Did you know this? I didn't. It strikes me as a thing the country ought to be known for, and yet, being the sixth most populous country in the world is likely not what comes to mind when most Americans think of Nigeria. When I was growing up, it seemed my dad's Home was a country best known for Nigerian prince email scams.

With the more recent impact of social media, Nigerians are able to redefine this negative image for themselves. So perhaps today when you think of Nigeria, you think of beautiful and lavish weddings, dance, and music. And yet: those colloquial efforts to alter the country's image aren't strong enough to overcome the US State Department's pinned Google search result that warns Americans thinking about tourism to Nigeria to "reconsider travel." Even today, when I google "how is Nigeria perceived," my search results are peppered with words like "corruption" and "failure," and articles about the country's image crisis.

Then again: maybe Google is just reinforcing a story I already believe to be true.

11. When I ask my mom about where my dad is from, she will tell me Uyo, Nigeria. This is true in the way that a person who is from Arlington saying they are from Boston is "true," although Arlington is an independent municipality about six miles north of Boston. It is true in the way that I will say I am from Milwaukee, when I actually lived in Mequon: a twenty-five-minute drive and twenty miles north of the city. My dad was actually born and raised in Ikot Okure: a small eastern Nigeria village in the state of Akwa Ibom. Ikot Okure is ten miles east of Uyo, the state capital, and an eleven-hour drive from Lagos.

When you look up Ikot Okure on Google Maps, the answer you get—of course—depends on what Google believes to be the answer you seek. You might find the location of the Roman Catholic church, which comes as no surprise to me as I've always known my dad once studied to be a priest in that church. Or you may find nothing at all.

Which: also comes as no surprise to me.

Nigeria is home to hundreds of tribes who speak at least double that amount of languages, and like Ghana,[12] Nigeria was also colonized by the British. Since our colonial overlords speak English: English is the official language of both countries and my parents' only shared language. Similar to the United States and Ghana: in Nigeria, Christians rank in the majority, with indigenous or traditional religion practitioners making up a small minority.[13]

Nigeria's flag was designed by the 1959 contest winner, Michael Taiwo Akinkunmi, and first officially raised on October 1, 1960. The Nigerian flag features a white stripe (peace and unity) with green stripes (natural wealth) to each side. But, much like the story I remember reading about Ghana's flag, alterations were also made to Nigeria's winning flag design. Akinkunmi's original flag featured a bright red sun in its center—which was later removed by the Nigerian government. I did not struggle to make metaphor of this fact. Red is the color of blood, and blood was removed[14] from the very center of the public symbol of where my dad is from. It was almost too on the nose—my life is that metaphor.

12. Someone once asked me if you could drive from Accra to Lagos, and I laughed because I did not know the answer. When I asked Google, I was warned that the route has tolls and crosses through multiple countries, and that the destination is in a different time zone. Also: the route was closed and there were no other routes. "Check conditions before you go," Google told me—echoing the State Department's more direct suggestion to reconsider going at all.

13. This is, at least, what Google will tell you. But my understanding of the story is not quite so clearly delineated. My dad's tribe, the Ibibio, are believed to be the earliest inhabitants of southern Nigeria. They are a religiously complicated community, in that the Ibibio simultaneously practice and deeply believe in Christianity *and* indigenous religions.

14. My third-grade teacher recently asked if I have ever visited Nigeria. I have been to Ghana twice: once to lay flowers on my grandmother's grave and once just to visit—and I plan to return again. But no: I have never visited Nigeria. And even if the State Department and Google were to modify their precautions about travel there, I likely never will.

In my memory, my mother taught me to draw a star so that I could create a Ghanaian flag during the inevitable "Heritage Week" in 1990s American schools. But I cannot remember ever drawing the Nigerian flag, nor ever claiming it as my own. Still: I feel intensely protective of Nigeria. While I wasn't raised to know much about where my dad came from, I don't like when people talk shit about his homeland. I make an effort to not talk shit about Nigeria, to not homogenize nor demonize an entire country because of my one, solitary, family story. And: I am certain I have failed.

There is a long, complicated political history between Ghana and Nigeria. While my parents were getting married in a Milwaukee church in 1979, droves of Ghanaians were migrating to Nigeria. And by the time I was born in 1983, about a million Ghanaians had been expelled from Nigeria, followed by another several hundred thousand in the next two years. But this history was never a discussion around our kitchen table in suburban Wisconsin. In fact, my parents never really spoke about their Homes at all. As an adult, social media would teach me of the decades-long rivalry over Nigerian versus Ghanaian jollof rice, but all I ever remember us eating was Rice-A-Roni—the San Francisco Treat settling any would-be debates between whether flavors are best served on basmati or long grains. It didn't matter to me what was going on outside of our home. As a kid, the only Ghanaian and Nigerian I saw on a daily basis loved each other deeply, with no rivalry to speak of.

Still: I want to be a writer who has so thoroughly researched her own life that I could succinctly summarize the international relations between Ghana and Nigeria. I am not, however, that writer. And I guess that's okay. Because the truth is: This book is not a story about Ghana and Nigeria. This book is my story.

Just about anyone on my mom's side of the family can tell me stories about the Yarneys and Ghana, and I believe the stories they tell me—with or without further verification. But outside of what my mom can tell me, almost everything I know about Nigeria comes from the internet—which has already proven itself an unreliable narrator. And almost everything I know about my dad's family and how he was raised comes from his favorite nephew, Eman, who my dad sponsored to come to America and live with us in the early 1990s.

Eman can tell me what my dad's parents did for a living. He can tell me how—despite having no formal education—

they were successful entrepreneurs who were well regarded in the community. He can tell me that my dad's mom lived until about the age of ninety, and that my dad's dad lived until the age of ninety-two.

Longevity, Eman tells me, runs in my dad's family. But: this is a story I struggle to believe.

When I speak to Cousin Eman about my dad's family, I have to practice saying the word "our" in my head before I say it out loud, making sure my mind will be able to choke the term past my throat. I struggle to refer to Eman's mother as my "aunt," but Eman naturally refers to my dad's parents as "our grandparents." It is easy for him, and why wouldn't it be? They *are* his family, and there is no challenge to him in claiming that.

I cannot relate.

I lived in the same house as Eman for several years of my childhood, and yet: prior to setting out to write this book, I could not have told you his mother's name. I could not have told you how many siblings my dad had, and generally speaking: I knew so little about the Okokon side of my family tree that sometimes I even questioned if I was pronouncing my own name correctly. Oh-KOH-kin, I enunciate when asked how to say my father's family's name. OHH-koh-kin, oh-KON-KON, oh-KON-kin others will mis-parrot back to me. Sometimes they say it with such confidence, I wonder if everyone else knows a truth about me that I have never learned.

My dad is one of six siblings and one half sibling. The eldest sibling is his half sister, Macy, and his parents then had six children together: Petronila (Eman's mom), Africanus (my dad), Affi, Theresa, Grace, and Thomas. When Eman tells me this, I scribble their names into my notebook, like an official registry of my ancestry. And now, years later, I type the names into my computer screen to be included in this book: as though having it printed will make it official. As though their names in my book will make them my family. Serve as evidence of somehow greater weight than the fact that I've never met a single one of these people, and likely never will.

Petronila? I ask, having Eman repeat his mother's name, so I can parrot it back to him to make sure I am pronouncing it correctly. Peh-tro-KNEEL-yahhh. I have never even heard this series of syllables before.

As I stare at this list of names in my notebook—my frantically drawn family tree—the page feels filled with strangers, unfamiliar. I wonder if any of them have a notebook where they wrote down the names of me and my mom and my siblings. I wonder, if faced with a list of our shared names, would we seem like strangers to them too?

In writing this book, I learned there is so much about my own history that I have never heard before. There are stories I have never been told, details I've never been invited to believe, and facts I will never be able to verify. In writing this book, I learned that I get to decide how this story is told.[15]

---

15. More of that later.

PART ONE

LOVE LETTERS

I 've been told (usually as a precursor to a pending breakup) that I am "a lot." I feel big, I talk loud, and I have strongly held opinions on plenty of entirely inconsequential things (Do you think the kind of glassware a bar serves your drink in doesn't matter? Well, you're wrong. Please allow me to share this PowerPoint presentation I've prepared on the subject). Lizzo's lyrics "All my feelings Gucci (it's Gucci)" from her song "Exactly How I Feel" are tattooed down the side of my left arm, which is to say that I—quite literally—wear my feelings on my sleeve. Maybe it's a lot, but this is just who I am, and as far as I'm concerned: This is who I've always been. I'm gonna show up. I'm gonna tell you how I feel. I'm gonna keep being here until you reject me, and then I'm probably gonna write about it on Facebook, tell about it in a story, or publish it in an essay so the whole world will know how I'm feeling.

My mom has always told me that I was *such a good baby*, one she describes as easygoing, easy to put to bed. I never cried too much unless I was hungry, and—before being potty-trained—I was known to silently find a corner in a room or crawl underneath a nearby table, turn my back to the rest of the world, and poop my diaper in private. It isn't lost on me that my mom's definition of a "good baby" is just to say that I was quiet and either didn't have a lot of needs or didn't express them much. But I mean . . . I can't say I agree with the interpretation that "good" means "doesn't speak up for herself." Still, all things considered, I was a generally happy baby who met most developmental milestones as were to be expected. Except—I didn't start talking until I was three. My parents weren't worried about it. *She'll talk when she's ready*, they said.

I think a lot about what parts of my identity exist because someone has *told* me that this is what I'm like; versus me believing from the inside that this is who I am. Like can you remember the first time you heard a recording of your own voice? I thought I sounded like one of the Chipmunks, but everyone else insisted that my voice sounded perfectly normal, just like how I always sound. So which reality is real? Or maybe both are true. Maybe I—at the same time—am an "a lot" woman who wears her heart on her sleeve, who shows up, tells her story publicly, and seeks connection to others; and I am also that little girl who was easygoing, slow to speak, and seeking to experience her most personal moments in private.

·   ·   ·

My big sister, Veronica, was a thumb-sucker, and our parents spent hours worrying about her teeth bucking forward and anxious that her bad habit would rub off on me via observation. At that age, Veronica and I had a typical big sister/little sister relationship: I constantly wanted to be around her, and she generally regarded me as a nuisance—a shadow, a pest who was always trying to get into her business. Our parents were right to worry that I might take up sucking my thumb, because for me, Veronica was everything, and anything she was doing was something I wanted to do too. Veronica loved playing with Barbies, so I liked playing with Barbies. Veronica's favorite color was green, so I covered every page of my coloring books with scribbles of green crayon. Veronica loved her

Blankie, so I, too, wanted to be near Blankie—consequences be damned.

Just before I started speaking, I had my first and only bone break. It happened because I was standing on Veronica's baby blanket. Outraged that I would disrespect Blankie in this way, Veronica—two years my senior, so about four or five at the time—yanked Blankie out from underneath me and I fell, the weight of my toddler body crashing onto my chubby little right arm, breaking the bones within. I'm sure I cried, waited for my mom to come and pick me up, and then perhaps felt a tinge of shame for getting Veronica a scolding. Even if it was her fault, I never wanted to get anyone else in trouble, least of all my big sister.

It would be days before my mom—a pediatrician(!)—would notice my arm was broken. You see, back home in Ghana, kids were trained to do things with their right hand, as the left hand was considered dirty and reserved for wiping one's butt after pooping. Both Mom and Uncle Ato have almost identical handwriting, possibly because they were both hit with the same rulers over their knuckles for writing left-handed in school. A few days after Veronica pulled Blankie out from underneath me, Mom noticed I was feeding myself with my left hand. *Hmm . . .* she said to herself, *I thought that kid was right-handed.*

I imagine a slow-motion vignette of the last few days began to play in her mind. The montage ends with her walking into a room and seeing me lying on the ground, body weight over my right arm, crying, while Veronica sits happily, thumb and a tuft of Blankie stuffed into her mouth.

Like many stories of my childhood, this one has become something of a family lore. When my mom tells this story now, she recounts it with a smile, an almost twinkle in her eye as she laughs at the missteps of her younger self. Veronica tells it as a moment when she was mean to someone she loves—it's become a story she uses for teaching lessons to her kids and children's therapy clients. I tell it as a testament to how much I love my big sis. The story of me, Veronica, and Blankie has been told and retold so many times that it almost feels like a memory for me, but I am perhaps the only person involved in the story who does not have any actual memory of it happening.

The year would have been about 1985, back before we lived with a camera in our hands or back pockets at all times, ready to capture and semi-publicly archive every seemingly meaningful moment of our lives. No one was there to document that my arm breaking happened the way we all say it did. No one snapped a photo of my snapping limb, in fact: I can't recall ever even seeing an image of myself with a cast on my arm. I know it happened because my family tells me it did—and I believe them.

I believe that I didn't start talking until I was three. I believe that my arm was broken. And I believe that I was an easy baby, despite the fact that "easygoing" is not an adjective I would ever pick to describe what I know of the woman I have become. Because that's the thing about identity: So much of it is nothing more than what others see in you. Your voice is normal, not a Chipmunk's voice, this is how you sound, who you are, who you've always been.

In the end, Veronica's thumb-sucking likely did contribute to her eventually needing braces, but I never sucked my thumb. I sucked my tongue instead. It was a quiet activity, one that didn't sound any orthodontist bill alarm bells, and it's something I continue to do to this day—often when I am trying to keep myself from saying what I really feel.

First you're laughing . . . then you're cryingggg, Veronica used to croon in a song she wrote about me. I was just your average second child—and a quick scroll through Google will tell you that we are rebellious peacemakers. Loners who want relationship. Troublemakers who want to please others. I want to be around you. I want you to want me to be there. But ultimately, I want it when and how I want it—on my own terms.

•   •   •

Veronica and I would create what felt like elaborate Barbie homes, cars, and entire neighborhoods that were—in reality—little more than a desk, a chair, and a couple of open-top shoeboxes. We furnished the homes with rolled-up washcloths stacked on discarded bracelet boxes for beds, pieces of cardboard wrapped with tinfoil for mirrors, and little white "tables" repurposed from Pizza Hut delivery boxes. Sometimes we played nice, and other times we would topple over each other's Barbie homes, rip up the other's shoebox car, or the ultimate offense: Give the other's Barbie a haircut (that *never* worked out well). But then we would talk it out, make up, and rebuild—together. Veronica was my first friend.

By the time I entered kindergarten, I was ready to make more friends. Veronica and our little sister, Affi, had taught me how to play nice with other kids, and I didn't have too hard of a time transferring those skills over to interactions in the schoolyard. But the butterflies that fluttered in my belly the first time I saw a kid named Justin—well, those took me by surprise.

Justin was my first crush. He was cute, short, and clear-skinned with brown hair. I mean, I suppose we were all clear-skinned and short back then—it was kindergarten, after all. What I liked most about Justin was that he would wear this one sweater: it was light brown and had green, red, blue, and maybe a few yellow brick-like block shapes woven into it. He was just so dang handsome in that sweater! And he was so nice! . . . Or, at least, his sweater was nice. Actually, now that I think about it, I remember very little about Justin beyond his sandy brown hair and his cozy-lookin' sweater. I knew about as much about Justin as future-me would know about any dude I'd eventually swipe right on, and literal marriages grow from Tinder, so suffice it to say: I knew enough to send the 1980s kindergarten version of a first message.

After a few weeks of school, I decided to write Justin a love letter. I *needed* to tell him how I felt. I wanted to write an ode to his sweater. A poetic waxing on the lesser-noticed nuances of his sandy brown bangs. It would be a declaration of the kind of love that grows in indoor sandboxes, reading nooks, and

LEGO corners. The only trouble was I couldn't write a love letter because I didn't know how to read or write.

Enter: my big sis. By now Veronica was in second grade, so certainly she could do this for me. Of course when I asked she said no, as big sisters are oft to do in response to the random requests of their kid-shadows. Maybe she was mad about some recently destroyed Barbie house, or maybe I'd let it slip to one of her very mature second-grade friends that she still slept with her Blankie. But like any kid sister, I was determined to get my way. I imagine it took several days—a lifetime to a kindergartener with a crush—but eventually: Veronica wrote my love letter.

The next day would have been a crisp autumn morning early on in the school year, just a few weeks before we would dress ourselves in costume and demand candy from strangers. I can see myself walking the short distance to Westside Elementary School with Veronica, love note hot in my hand and faith warm in my chest. I would have scouted Justin out from among the gaggle of blond- and brown-haired boys in our classroom and walked right up to him. No longer quite so easygoing, I'd developed into a confident, willful child, and if photos from that time are any indication: I was likely dressed in neon colors paired with zebra print, my natural hair pulled into a puff-pony perched on the top of my head.

Justin, on the other hand, was a shy kid. In fact, my attraction to shy folks who find me (hopefully! but more likely temporarily . . .) charmingly disorienting is a tendency that has carried through to my adulthood.

Justin received my note, and would have responded with a look of reluctance and confusion. Because, here's the thing: Justin was also in kindergarten. Which means that, like me, Justin *also* did not know how to read or write. He took the letter—my open heart spilled onto a page for the first time ever—turned around, marched right up to Mrs. Wilson, gave her the note, and turned me in. And just like that: my very first crush ended.

Theresa and the kindergarten love note is another of my family's lores, a story I've heard, told, and retold as though it were an actual memory in my own mind. Whenever I tell this story now, I recount it with a smile. An almost twinkle in my eye as I laugh at the missteps of my younger self. *Did it hurt? Were you sad? Did you cry??* people will ask me, and my response is invariably a shrug accompanied by a chuckled *No*. I was a child, it was a silly crush, and it's just a fun story about my past. I don't sit around wishing for the past to be different than it was, and there is no part of me left wondering—had things gone differently—if I'd have ended up married to some kid I met in kindergarten. I might have been temporarily embarrassed, but this is a *good* memory. A happy memory.

I think people ask me if Justin's rejection hurt because that is what they hear in the story. But just as my recorded voice sounds different to everyone else than it does to me— "hurt" is not what *I* hear. For me this is a story of triumph. It was the first time I had a big feeling about a person outside of my family, and I told them exactly how I felt. I think of it as a moment of me becoming who I am. I don't like to make the first move, but (to this day) I'm usually the one to make it because what I REALLY can't stand is not saying how I feel. I can suck my tongue for only so long, and then I'm gonna shoot my shot.

The last time I uttered the words "I love you" to a partner, he responded with "I know," and then changed the subject to make fun of me (again) for my insufficient *Star Wars* knowledge. There was a tinge of pain, but that was quickly overtaken by something that felt akin to good. Akin to happy. I think of that *Star Wars* moment the same way I do about my failed kindergarten love letter. The note I wrote to Justin was not about him. It wasn't even about his sweater. It was about me. Telling someone how I feel is always more about me than it is about them.

My current Google Drive still holds the last love letter I wrote, which is to say it was sent not too long ago. It was a tale as old as kindergarten: I wanted him, and he didn't want me back. The difference was, of course, that he had already made that clear. I had convinced myself that maybe—hopefully!—if I was able to find the perfect words to tell him exactly how I felt, he would feel differently. This time, I had told him I was going to write him a letter, and he had asked me not to. I did it anyway. I spilled my open heart onto a digital page, printed it out, and dropped it—sealed in a handwritten envelope—into the big blue box a few blocks from my home.

He never read it. Years later he moved halfway across the country (without telling me he was leaving), packed the still unopened letter into one of his moving boxes, and took it with him.

I want this to be a fun story of my past. A moment where I suffered a temporary schoolyard embarrassment, picked myself up, dusted myself off, and kept on moving. But it's not, and admittedly the tinge of hurt lasted longer this time. And yet: Not unlike the letter to Justin, this one was—ultimately—

a letter to myself. A declaration of *my* feelings. An opening of *my* heart. So in that way, it's almost fitting that I'm the only one who has ever read it.

That isn't to say that I am unfazed by rejection. Just like my big sister used to sing, I am laughing, until I'm crying. To an outsider looking in, I am living 100 percent out loud: being my honest and flawed self on social media and telling stories about my life in front of crowds of strangers. I am still the kid who will give you a love letter without thinking about whether or not you can read it. My heart may be permanently tatted on my sleeve, but I am still human. And so with each failed attempt to connect my heart to another, I've continued to grow a self-protective, external sheath of armor that has become, ever increasingly, more and more hardened. As a result, I've become less and less likely to genuinely believe that it's safe to tell anyone how I feel. Justin rejecting my kindergarten love letter perhaps should have taught me that it's safer to hold back. But the lesson never stuck—armor be damned.

It is not smart, nor safe, nor well-advised to write your feelings down on paper and give them to another person, having no assurance that they will hear you the way you intend to be heard—and yet here I am, writing this book.

Since learning how to express myself I haven't really learned how to stop. And for many (perhaps even most?) I am still "a lot." But this isn't a flaw I want to fix—in fact, despite a lifetime of evidence and experience to the contrary, I don't even see it as a flaw.

I want to be near you. I want you to want me to be there. But I am not interested in being who you want—or believe—me to be. I'd rather tell you, show you, who I am. And heads up: the going will not be easy.

MEET-CUTE

When I was twenty-two and in my first job out of college, a newlywed coworker told me she'd met her husband on Yahoo! Personals.

You should try it! she enthused. *It worked for me!!*

This was 2005: the same year YouTube, Reddit, and Etsy were founded, but nearly a decade before Tinder or Bumble would swipe their ways into our there-is-no-other-way-to-meet-people reality. Other than this coworker, I didn't know anyone who'd met a life partner online and it seemed like a dangerous and sketchy idea because I wasn't trying to get chopped up or left for dead in some abandoned van down by the Fox River in Green Bay, Wisconsin. *It's not like meet-*

ing men on Craigslist, she convinced me. *These are real, normal guys who are looking for love just like you are.*

I took her advice and eventually met Patrick, who would become the first in a nearly two-decades-long string of online boyfriends. Once, Patrick made me eggs Benedict with homemade hollandaise sauce and fresh strawberries. When I met his mom, she couldn't stop gushing about how beautiful I was, and I couldn't stop wondering if she was trying to say she thought I was out of Patrick's league, or if she was trying to let me know she was okay with her White son dating a Black woman. Patrick and I lasted about a month, maybe two. I think he got scared off after my friends—drunk on what we called "Boone's Punch," mixed in a bucket in our garage—tried to jump on his sensible Prius and catch us kissing in the front seat.

Since then it's been almost all online for me: eHarmony, Match, OkCupid, Tinder, Bumble, Hinge—you name it. I can't count the number of first dates I've been on, nor can I count the number of men I've slept with without pulling up the Notes app on my cell phone to double-check my memory. My dating life has become little more than a scrolling list of solitude broken up by one-night stands, flings, and flops that never last longer than it takes to incubate a full-term human. But with the exception of a three-ish-year gap from age thirty-seven to forty (which I would like to blame on the pandemic but was really more about my realizing I maybe needed to be single for a while) I have never stopped trying.

Part of my practice is to always ask couples how they met. It's almost like an anthropological study for me, and I hope that maybe—in one of their stories—I might just find some direction on what I've been doing wrong all this time.

High school? Check. Went there, no lasting sweethearts.

College? Yea . . . TBH I'm glad *that* one didn't work out.

The grocery store? Well, girl's gotta eat, so . . . Check!

When I decided I wanted to write a book, I took a class. I learned about craft, and I learned about the publishing industry, and I learned the steps you take to get to where I am now. Same goes for when I decided I wanted to buy a house: There are steps, and I sought to learn them. With either process, everyone told me that it was going to take time. That I should prepare myself to have lots of rejected offers before I found "the one." And once I did, there would still be more steps to go through. Home inspection, appraisal, final approval, closing (or, in the case of book publishing: editing, thinking you're done, editing, and then editing some more). There is a system, a process, an agreed-upon protocol to follow. When I ask couples how they met, I'm trying to understand "The Dating System." Teach me the steps, tell me the rules, and put me in, Coach: I'm ready!

There was a time in my life when I believed that romantic love was guaranteed. As a kid, I knew only one uncoupled adult (my godmother), and from the story my mom seemed to be telling me, Auntie Marie was single by choice. My parents had found love. The rest of my aunties and uncles had found love. All of my friends' parents had too. Love seemed to be a birthright, and I had no reason to believe it wouldn't happen for me.

But after nearly two decades of failure, I've begun to wonder if I took a wrong turn and missed my chance to course correct. Maybe "the one" was three rows behind me in biology class, two aisles over at the grocery, or one more swipe on some app. Maybe I haven't been following the right steps or putting in the right kind of work in the right kind of way to earn the one thing that has always felt just outside of my reach. From being a Peace Corps Volunteer to a yoga teacher to a writer: I've never been the kind of person who follows a clearly charted path, but

I've always managed to find my way to wherever I was trying to go. Except when it comes to romance. And I can't help but wonder if I've unknowingly mis-navigated: driving myself forever and ever further and further in the wrong direction.

．．．

I once had a second date take me to see a scary movie, and then chastise me for being scared. *If I'd known you were gonna cover your eyes half the time*, he complained, *I would've asked for a discount ticket.* I decided not to see him again because dudes who fail to get to know me and then don't like what they find once they do are a dime a fucking dozen. But having shared interests is one of the repeated rules to The Dating System. *Do things you love, and you'll find someone who loves them too*, they say.

I . . . am not convinced. I've gone to plenty of storytelling shows, bookstores, and bougie cocktail joints, and then I go home alone. I've been looking up Kurt Vonnegut or Anthony Bourdain since the days when Bing was my go-to search engine, only to be reminded that I don't care about them any more than I care if my partner and I like reading the same kinds of books or stan the same celebrity chefs. I can't imagine expecting anyone to suffer through a formulaic rom-com or all forty-seven hundred episodes of the latest season of *Love Island* with me—much less finding someone who *wanted* to do those things, like voluntarily. The idea of finding someone who likes doing the things I like to do is nice and all, but I mean: Do I really *like* watching *The Bachelorette*? No. Was I absolutely invested in Team Gabby? That's a hard yes. Honestly, it sort of amazes me when couples bond over a shared taste in books or movies or TV, and I've always kind of figured that maybe this rule just doesn't apply to me.

Love comes when you least expect it, they say. *My husband is a date I almost didn't go on!* A steadfast commitment to never wanting too much, yet never giving up, is another one of The Dating System rules. Well, let me tell you: I regularly go to Trader Joe's in my pajamas—ready to be surprised by some good-looking stranger—and I've never left with anything more than green goddess seasoning and soft strawberry licorice (not that I'm complaining, oh Trader Joe's gawds, please don't discontinue my favorites!). I've gone on plenty of dates I wasn't actually interested in or didn't actually want to go on, and most times the best part of the night was my perfectly cooked salmon dinner. Delux Cafe with that one comedian who—without knowing much more than my name—told me I was everything he'd been looking for. Brookline's Regal Beagle with the guy who refused to go dutch by way of offering to show me his tax return to prove he made more money than me. The washed-up wannabe rocker who ordered a Pabst and asked zero questions about me at the Middle East in Central Square. I could guide a Duck Tour of Greater Boston, detailing all the lackluster dates I've been on.

On the other hand, halfway through her senior year in college, my little sister, Affi, drew up a road map for her life, and then tucked it away in the back of her closet. The plan was that she would graduate and, shortly thereafter, meet and fall in love with her eventual husband. They would date, they would marry, and then she would enroll in and complete graduate school to become a children's therapist. She and her husband would have babies, buy a house, and then retire in Ghana. When Affi met her future husband out dancing one night with her girlfriends, he was right on time. Everything else fell into place just as she'd planned.

With or without a map, this is how it's gone for everyone in my immediate family—except for me. My parents met in their twenties, and all three of my siblings met their spouses around the age of twenty-five. But when I was that age, I was in the Peace Corps and falling in love with what felt like endless possible versions of my eventual life. I dated while I was living in Ecuador, and sure: we talked about marriage just like any love-struck twentysomething couple does. But by the time I was heading back home to midwestern America, we'd broken up.

Just be yourself! they say—another one of the oft-repeated rules of The Dating System. My siblings taught me how to be a good friend, but I never really learned how to be a good girlfriend, perhaps in no small part because it's taken me so many years to learn who I even am in the first place. I have friends who married (and stayed with!) their high school sweethearts, but honestly: I wouldn't have fallen in love with teenage-me either. I'll give her some grace for age-appropriate, hormone-related behavior, but generally speaking: She was a wreck of a person. At that age, I still—quite fundamentally—lacked a sense of self, and I took my uncomfortable ambiguity out on everyone around me. I didn't know that being me was something I would have to learn how to do, and it would take me even longer to realize that love is a learned behavior too.

I was thirty-three when Affi got married. Coming off a failed nine-month-long relationship with a guy who would—

eventually—go on to marry the next woman he dated, I flew into Milwaukee for the ceremony. I'm sure there was a part of me who thought I might meet someone at the wedding (or better yet at the airport like the main character in some 1990s rom-com!) but I cannot genuinely recall ever being the type who thought her love life might contain any elements of movie magic.

That weekend, I got mani-pedis with my mom, despite the fact that I hate getting my nails done. Nail polish makes my fingernails feel heavy, and I was only in the habit of getting pedicures because when I'd shown up to my first yoga teacher training, I'd realized that all of the other teachers-in-training had candy-colored toenails. It was an expensive habit that I didn't even enjoy, but this was my little sister's wedding—a special occasion—and we were all going full out. My mom (despite the fact that she *also* suffers from the same heavy-nail-bed sensation as I do) wanted to get her nails done. And I (remembering that love is a learned behavior) agreed to go with her.

I just think this might be my last chance, my mom said, looking down at the pedicurist massaging her calves. *Last chance for what?* I asked, wincing as my pedicurist clipped one of my stubborn cuticles. *You know, to see one of my kids get married,* she said as she looked over at me, an eyebrow raised, her expression carrying an equal-parts mix of hope and giving up.

I snort-laughed. *Oh? I'm sure Africanus and his girlfriend will get married someday.*

Well, she retorted, *this might be my last chance to be the mother of the briiiide.*

Yeah. I laughed, trying not to jolt my whole body and kick the pedicurist in the nose. *You are probably right about that one,* I said, followed by: *So live it up now while ya can, Madre!,* trying to lighten the mood.

I'm sure there was a part of me who was hurt to hear my mother say this. But (outside of what was happening with my cuticles) "hurt" was not the dominant feeling I experienced at the time. Sure, I was older than anyone in my family had ever been by the time they'd met "the one." And yeah, I was in town that weekend to witness my *younger* sister get married. And . . . okay, I *had* spent the last month allowing a parade of nothing-but-names-in-my-Notes-app men lick my proverbial wounds after my most recent breakup. But don't they say you gotta kiss a lot of frogs before you find your prince? Maybe my frog catalog was just a bit longer than most others'.

Every relationship you're ever in will fail, until the one that doesn't, they say. This might be the only rule I actually appreciate, because it's the only one of The Dating System's rules that convinces me I might not be doing anything wrong. I'm just living my life. Dating all the wrong ones until I meet the right one.

If I'm honest, though, sitting in that nail salon at the age of thirty-three, I was quietly beginning to lose hope that love would ever actually happen for me. But I was nowhere near admitting this out loud. Especially not to my mom, and least of all: to myself. I was able to slough off what my mom said that day as easily as my pedicurist was able to deal with the cracked and dry skin on the bottom of my feet because, be it your heart or your heels: This is what happens when you misuse and refuse care. You begin to dry up, and what's underneath begins to go numb.

There is an episode of *Black Mirror* (a show I watch only if my big sister previews the episode and deems it "not too scary" for me to check out) where people can opt in to a place actually called "the System." It is a simulated soulmate-finding experience where everyone has a palm-size, handheld device called "Coach," who directs them on what their next date will be. At any point of each coupling, the pair can ask Coach how long their relationship will last. Two hours. Twelve hours. Three months, five months, one year, forever. They can, if they so choose, know from the jump how long the gig is gonna take. And then the couple can decide what to do with that information.

Often what they do is bang one out before the timer goes off. And—after a series of short bang-out stints—the episode's lead character says she doesn't even feel connected to her body anymore. Numbed out, she would watch her body go through the steps and wait for the System's big promise: the one. *It's just a dick going in and out of a hole*, she says.

Killing me softly, I replied out loud to no one, alone in my bed and propped up against my husband pillow with a bowl of popcorn and a glass of red wine.

I've come to refer to dating as "dinner with a stranger." It often feels like I am slowly removing my skin in hopes that the other person will be kind enough to not carelessly puncture my fleshy insides. I hate it. At times, dating has served the purpose of helping me get to know my new city; but going on a bunch of first dates as a vehicle to a lifelong partnership seems, honestly, bonkers to me. I cannot possibly be expected to remove my flesh this many times and then still walk away whole, unharmed, and with enough energy to redress myself and try it all over again the next weekend.

You'll find the one eventually! they say—and holding on to this belief is an essential rule of The Dating System. Keep trying. Keep hoping. Keep being open. But what the Coupled don't seem to understand is that being single is literally exhausting. All of the trying and failing breaks my spirit and makes me insurmountably sad. I am so, so, so tired, and I'm just not sure I have it in me to keep baring myself for relationships that don't last long enough to grow a fully baked human life. But the alternative reality of dying alone terrifies me. It floods my eyes and chokes my throat and fills me with a bottomless, hollow sense of paralyzing, panicked sorrow. Never finding love is one of my worst nightmares.

But you have so much love in your life already! a tarot reader once told me after pulling a card, making a strained face, and slamming the card—facedown—back onto her tapestry-covered table. *Just look around you,* she said, gesturing to three of my best friends sitting in a semicircle behind me.

Tell me what the fucking card says, thirty-four-year-old-me replied, my tone an equal-parts mix of demand and restraint. Only a year had passed since pedicures with my mom, and the loss of hope creeping over me was becoming increasingly difficult to deny.

The tarot lady inhaled. *I call it the "fuckboys card,"* she said on an exhale, slowly turning it back over. The Nine of Wands depicted a group of young men aimlessly swinging phallic sticks taller than their own bodies. I exhaled. Familiar, hot, tired tears welled behind my eyes, and I semi–blacked out her explanation about my battle for love being one that was yet to be completed anytime soon. Years later, my childhood babysitter would make a Facebook post about an online psychic who could tell you when you were destined to meet your soulmate. I laughed at the absurdity of such a thing and then immediately forked over $19.99 for my result. It's not like I actually believed it would work, but I also don't *actually* believe that vegetables can taste like meat and yet I've still purchased Impossible Burgers at Trader Joe's more than once.

The online psychic emailed me a pencil sketch of an average, racially ambiguous-looking dude and a note about how, for now, our "vibrational levels weren't aligned and calibrated towards meeting each other."

Jesus fucking Christ, I said out loud to no one. *Even this fake online psychic won't pretend to tell me when it will happen.*

As apprehensive as I was to meet men from the internet in the early days of Yahoo! Personals, holy moly, what I wouldn't do now for a System Coach or a soulmate psychic. At least that way I might know where to look. I might have someone to give me directions, to tell me what I've been doing wrong. Someone to tell me if I should keep trying or just give up.

Perhaps the most paramount of all rules from The Dating System is my least favorite rule of all. *The single most important decision any person will make is who they marry.* I hear this one all the time (most notably on an episode of a TLC show about a man with four wives). I was maybe thirty-six years old when I decided to text my mom and ask what *she* thought was the most important decision *her* kids would make in their lives. I was sure she'd say something about choosing a major in college, deciding where to live as an adult, or I don't know—buying a Toyota rather than an American-made car.

Who they marry, my mom responded within minutes.

But . . . But what about me? I asked.

I'm sure there was a part of me who was hurt to receive this response from my mother. But honestly, "hurt" was still not my dominant emotion at the time. Not because it didn't hurt my feelings; rather, this time it was because I had gone fully numb.

Just like that tarot card reader, the Coupled are always quick to remind me how much love I already have in my life; how successful and accomplished I am. But—with or without my mom's text or the opinion of some guy whose wives would all (but one) eventually leave him—I know that none of that really matters. I can publish a book, and I can get every job I seek on my winding and uncharted path. My bank can even preapprove me as a single person for a mortgage: And still none of it will matter if I die having never made the most important decision a person can ever make. I stan Liz Phair, but she was wrong about shitloads of money being all anyone really wants for themselves and their friends. What most of us want—for ourselves and for anyone else—is happiness. Fulfillment. Joy. And *that* would require lots of love.

But I cannot articulate for you—nor even hardly imagine for myself—what the love I seek might look like. So maybe that's what I've been doing wrong: maybe you can't expect to find what you're looking for if you can't even describe it.

. . .

When I was thirty-nine, my mom told me she believes there are people who are just not meant to find love, and that that was okay. She didn't name any names, but I knew who she was talking about. People like Auntie Marie. People like me.

I'd like to tell you that "hurt" was not my dominant emotion after hearing her say this. I'd like to tell you that hearing it reminded me that I am a strong, independent, happy, and fulfilled woman. I would even like to tell you that I was too numb to feel anything at all.

But all of those things would be lies.

The truth is: My mom's words punctured like a shiv to my exposed and fleshy insides, and I couldn't look her in the eye because it felt like she had finally given up. Called off the search party and declared my love life as presumed dead. The only aid I could render to the blood gushing from this fresh wound was knowing that my mom was trying to tell me that—whether or not I was ready to admit it to myself—I hadn't done anything wrong.

And I *want* to believe that. I want to believe that The Dating System rules might someday work for me too. More than anything, I want to believe that I can die happy whether or not I ever find the love I am seeking. But I would be lying if I told you that I consistently find the strength to believe any of those things. I'd be lying if I said I genuinely believe I haven't done anything wrong, just as much as I'd be lying if I said I knew what to do to get it right.

When someone dies, you mourn them. You accept that the possibility of seeing them again in this life is gone, and you find a way to move forward knowing that they will never be part of your future. And at some point, you have to stop being actively sad about it.

But I would be lying if I told you that I have mourned—or even begun to fully accept—the reality that my attempts at following The Dating System rules might not ever work out for me.

ME LLAMO THERESA

On the inside of my right ankle sits the lowercase letter *t*. It's not often visible to passersby, but every once in a while it will provoke a comment. *Is that an anchor?* (No.) *Are you very passionate about tea and abbreviations?* (No.) *Is it so you don't forget your name?*

I got the tattoo as a sober decision after a drunken night. Many of my evenings, especially on the weekends during my first year after college, were spent in a local gay bar in Green Bay, Wisconsin. The bar was called XS, and we were regulars. The owner, who also worked as a bartender, knew upon seeing me to start mixing up my favorite drink, the Stop n' Go. The drink had Midori liqueur at the bottom—a heavy syrup cordial that allowed a layer of pineapple juice to sit above it—

and a layer of cranberry mixed with vodka sat on the very top. Green, yellow, red: the Stop n' Go.

One evening, a woman came in and she had the letter *E* on her shoulder. It was curvy and scripty, and I loved it immediately. Her name started with an *E*, maybe Erica or Emily, and that's why she had the tattoo. I pointed it out to my friends, semi-drunkenly exclaiming, *Wouldn't it be fun if we all got our initials tattooed? We could all go together and do it at the same time!*

I've always loved the idea of group tattoos. I see them like a voluntary, forever inclusion—but individualized, and unique on each one's skin. My friends all agreed to the idea: there were almost a dozen of us who planned to get this done together. *C, K, T, E, J, Z, E, R, B*, and *T*. Becky loved drawing our names on sheets of paper for us to hang in our office spaces at work, and she determined it would be her role to draw all of the letters for our tattoos. Many days later, after everyone had sobered up, only three of us remained committed to the plan. *R, B*, and me: *T*. We scheduled the appointment and went in for our group tattoo.

It was my second tattoo, the first being a slightly altered version of Picasso's *Dove of Peace*, and it had not occurred to me that I would be asked to answer why I got it. No one had ever questioned my decision to brand myself with a marking of peace.

Like many kids, perhaps especially those socialized to be girls, I used to spend a lot of time thinking about my future kids' names. The bright pink box for Barbie's sister proclaimed her name as Skipper, but when I got a Skipper doll for my birthday one year, I renamed her Keys because I thought it was more unique. It was the name I planned to give out once I had a daughter of my own, and this redheaded, cream-skinned, plastic toy gave me a place to test-drive it. My Cabbage Patch doll was named Victor. When I got him for Christmas, my sisters and I immediately peeked under his shorts to see if he had a penis (he didn't; his crotch was just a single stitch, the same as the girl Cabbage Patch dolls they had received). Victor had brown skin just like mine, and he wore a crisp white shirt with a yellow collar and green shorts. As though it were a prophecy directly from the toy factory, I decided my future son would one day be called Victor too.

I am named for my dad's favorite sister, Aunt Theresa, about whom I have always known but two precious facts. The first is that she once bought a goat in my honor. When my dad told me this as a kid, I thought, *Well, that's an odd thing to do: buy me a goat on the other side of the world.* It's not like I could snuggle it or play with it. It's not a pet, my dad would have told me, it's for food, and, eventually, they did slaughter and eat it. When my dad told me about the slaughter, he said it with an excited, reverent pride, as this, too, had been done in my honor.

I never met the goat, and I never met my aunt Theresa either. Because the other fact about her is that she, like all of my dad's family with the exception of my cousin Eman, would eventually cease all communication with me, my siblings, and my mom. Not even my name was enough of a peace offering to maintain a relationship with my now silent namesake.

All of this is to say I have very little connection to the series of syllables that spill out of a person's mouth when they look in my direction to start speaking. I'm a girl who doodled her name in the margins of her notebooks, who named her dolls in anticipation of her future children, who branded the initial *t* into her skin. And yet the name Theresa is, at best, an assignment not connected to my identity. While I was given my name by my dad, I feel about it the way my mom has always felt about hers.

. . .

Winneba is about thirty-five miles west of Accra, the capital of Ghana. It is a smallish city about the size of Oshkosh, Wisconsin, and there, at some point in the early 1950s, two neighbors were embroiled in a feud. This disagreement was over a seemingly simple thing so many neighbors disagree over: land. Where one person's stops, and the next person's begins. Like most neighborly disputes, this one was eventually resolved amicably. But unlike most, at the end of this argument one of the neighbors decided to name his next-born child after the previously disgruntled neighbor, a White woman named Enid Wells. The man, a Black Ghanaian and royalty in his Fante tribe, was my grandfather. As luck would have it, his next-born child was my mother. And so, my mom received her name, Enid Wells Yarney, by way of a peace offering over the placement of a driveway.

Perhaps because of these origins, my mom never really connected with her name. She seems to regard it as a formality, an obligation; we all have to have one and this one was directed to her. This might be why my mom didn't have names planned for her kids. She never test-drove the names of her future chil-

65

dren on her dolls, never doodled in any margins. She never had a list of names she was hesitant to tell her friends about, worried those friends would have children first and steal the name Taylor or Olivia or Sophia before she could claim it.

Lucky for my mom, my dad was a lot like George Foreman. He believed *all* of his children should have his name. My dad went by "Rick" to his classmates and later with his colleagues, but his name was Africanus. And so, my name is Africanus.

My father had a method for naming his daughters. The first name is an English—more specifically, Christian—name. This name was for formality's sake and was never meant to be used. The second name is a traditional Ibibio one, the name the daughter would be called. And finally, each girl's third name (and my brother's first name) would be his name, Africanus. Theresa, the name everyone now calls me, is my formal English name. The one that was never meant to be used.

It is common in my family to go by more than one name. My dad did it. My cousin Ekua used to go by Julie because it was easier for her coworkers to say; and my uncle Ato used to go by his first name, Rich, at times when he owned a business in Milwaukee. I knew my mom went by Enid to her coworkers, but when family visited, everyone called her Auntie Kukua. It was normalized that this was a thing that grown-ups did—have two names. It did not occur to me that I might one day follow in their rebranded lineage.

My middle name is Ini-Obong. My dad always told me this name means "God's Clock" or "God's Time." I am a woman who is habitually late, who arrives at destinations and goals on her own, entirely self-directed schedule—a woman who uses stories to unfreeze time—so I've always felt like my name was particularly well suited for me. When I was growing up, my family called me Ini for short. And while I don't know if any children feel a particular connection to their names, I was certainly the only Ini that I knew, so I for sure felt as though my name belonged to me.

River Falls, Wisconsin, was about one-fifth the size of Winneba and exactly the opposite in terms of the majority race of its population. It was 1989, and I was one of just two students of color among twenty-five to thirty kids in my kindergarten classroom, which was probably two more non-White students than most teachers at Westside Elementary School were accustomed to having. The other student of color was Korean, and when her mother gave her name to our teacher, Mrs. Wilson determined the name was too challenging to pronounce. The girl began to instead go by the name Meadow, since taking walks in the grassy park near her home was one of her favorite things to do.

When I imagine myself meeting Mrs. Wilson on my first day of kindergarten, I see a small, proud child. I am unscathed, unaware, and blissfully blind to what lies ahead of me. I am lifting the chin of my round brown face to meet Mrs. Wilson's eye. I am smiling. Feeling great about my first-day-of-school outfit. The breeze kisses my scalp in the sharply drawn parts between multiple ponytail twists done with so much care by my mom the night before—my crown of nappy hair tamed into careful sections, a barrette or a bally-ball tie at the end of each one. The plastic of my hair jewels clack against one another as I grin and announce myself as Ini.

All these years later, I can't say for certain how Mrs. Wilson's body responded to my name. But I imagine she would have cocked her head to the side, furrowed her brow a bit as she pursed her lips like she had tasted something sour. She removed her eyes from my proud gaze to look instead at my mother. *Is there anything else we can call her?* Mrs. Wilson asked. *Does she have a real name? An American name we can call her?*

Meadow's real name may have been difficult for this midwestern White woman's tongue, a tongue that somehow managed to learn how to shape itself into pronouncing words like the Wisconsin towns of Oconomowoc, Sheboygan, and Waukesha with accuracy, happy to learn how to twist correctly if for the sake of colonizing. But Ini is undeniably easy to pronounce. In fact, before having me in her classroom, I would be willing to bet that her tongue shaped up to allow *eenie, meenie, miney, mo* to spill from her lips a time or two when determining which kid would get to stand first in line or whose turn it was to sit on the favored carpet square during reading time. She had no reason to refuse my name. No reason other than that it was foreign to her, she was in charge, and she didn't have to say it if she didn't want to.

The name my mom offered to Mrs. Wilson on my first day of kindergarten was Theresa. It's my name, after all. But at the time, I didn't even know to answer to it. No one ever called me Theresa, so just as I had to learn my ABCs and my 123s, I had to learn to respond to my name. Mrs. Wilson paired me with Meadow—who was also learning to respond to her new name— and as classroom buddies, we quickly became best friends.

On my first day in Mrs. Wilson's classroom, I began to ex-

perience a particular type of identity crisis that so many immigrants and children of immigrants go through—where we
are called one name at school or at work, but another name at
home and in our hearts. It is the same crisis that led my cousin
to pull the name Julie from thin air, rebranding herself with
one of the names she may have had lined up for her daughters.
For my mother, this crisis began the moment my grandfather
needed to make peace with the White woman next door; my
mom's name is the consequence.

My dad's name—my name, my sisters' names, my brother's
name—literally means "African." But he, too, had this crisis,
offering the name Rick when he was so clearly proud of the
name Africanus that he would give it to all of his children. As
a child, I never thought about what it might be like for my son
Victor to tell the world he is named for his mother's penis-less
Cabbage Patch doll. But the names we give our children, the
syllables we offer when faced with the question of how to refer
to our flesh, do indeed have consequence. And whether they
intended to or not, by accommodating Mrs. Wilson with the
name Theresa, my parents passed along this crisis and consequence to me as much as they passed along the strength of a
name that could determine time.

Throughout my childhood, I tried on different nicknames, attempting to sand down Theresa into something that fit better within me. None of them stuck. I have a close friend named Elizabeth, and when asked if she goes by Liz or Beth for short, she says, *All of those, I go by all of those names.* I have always found it so curious. To have a name to which you so closely identify that any version of it still belongs to you.

In Spanish, one way to offer your name is to say, *Me llamo,* which means, *I call myself.* This resonates for me as a shrug, not a declaration. A noncommittal, not-quite-ownership of one's name. Today, I call myself Theresa, or sometimes just T. And perhaps my greatest peace offering, to myself and to everyone else, has been accepting this name and its consequence. I give this name so I keep getting invited into the conversation—because once friendships stop being arranged, people have to know what series of syllables to let spill from their lips should they decide to invite you into their conversation.

AIYSCH

I was four years old the first time we crossed the big blue bridge near the center of town, drove into a nice-looking neighborhood, and arrived at a split-level house on Sunset Lane. The house was tan colored when my parents first bought it, but my mom would agree to paint it light blue at our Realtor's advice, six years later when she put our home back on the market.

Next door and across a barrier of pine bushes was an older couple who didn't have any children. They grew rhubarb in their garden and would bake us pies every spring when the weather started to turn and the plant bloomed. We had a welcoming front yard, where my mom would plant flowers; and a wide and squat driveway, which opened into the garage. The garage's back door led to a space my parents called "the veranda"—which was really nothing more than a covered porch of bright green Astro-turf. When you stepped off the veranda, you entered a big back-yard. There was a giant white birch tree, a swing set, a sandbox, and plenty of space to run around with my siblings.

But when you walk into a split-level, it feels like you are arriving to nowhere. Split-levels greet you with a crossroads: a decision to go up or to go down. My memories of the house are split too.

We called the downstairs "the basement." It was semi-underground, but not scary like most basements were for me as a kid (and still are for me as an adult). It wasn't dark, damp, dusty, or unfamiliar. The basement was lived in. We had a big brown plaid couch, with cushions soft from years of use. Above a wooden cart sat a tube television—the old-school kind with a single, front-facing, visible speaker and faux-wood panels on the sides. Every winter, right next to the couch, we would assemble an artificial tree and decorate it with fragile tin balls and ornaments made in preschool classrooms from cheap ceramic and Popsicle sticks. We would take photos of us kids—my big sister, little sister, baby brother, and me—ripping into brightly wrapped boxes on Christmas morning, against the backdrop of the basement's wood-paneled walls.

The basement had a brown short-shag carpet, a fireplace with red bricks, and a built-in ledge where we would sit to pose for family photos. Once, my dad burned a bat in that fireplace. It entered our home through the garage and fluttered all over as we chased it; my mom crouched away in a corner to hide because she was terrified of bats. Eventually, my dad grabbed the fireplace poker tool, speared the bat, and charred it up in the fire. Then he took the burned-up bat body out onto the veranda. When I asked him why he was leaving it there, he said it was a warning to all other bats that ours was not a home they should dare to enter.

That's just the kind of guy my dad was. Practical, pragmatic, forward-thinking. He had a PhD in economics and was a professor at the University of Wisconsin–River Falls, whose campus sat just a few miles from our split-level home. But he was also known for dreaming out loud about one day opening a day care for kids. He planned to call it Future Investments because, he would say, *That's what kids are.* Maybe that's why—when an office on campus was redecorating—my dad brought home a bunch of old cubicles and installed them in the basement: giving us kids a formal and designated space to do our elementary school homework.

Just past the basement's fireplace was a little hallway with my parents' bedroom on the left and the laundry room on the right. Every year, as my mom slowly began to accumulate Christmas gifts, she would "hide" them in the laundry room before they were wrapped. As December approached, the shelves above the washer and dryer began to bulge with black Hefty bags, hardly concealing the sharp corners of Mattel and LEGO boxes. *If I see a bag with a rip in it*, Mom would say, *everything in that bag is going back to the store.* I'm sure there was a time when I believed Santa came down the split-level's chimney to arrive through the fireplace, but my mother's directives were no fantasy and no joke. I never dared peek into those bags.

At the top of the split-level's stairs hung a portrait of my family from before my brother was born. We are dressed in stiff, shiny clothing, and my little sister cradles a brown plastic baby doll, a compromise to keep her from crying at the sounds of shutters and the bright flashes in the photographer's studio at Sears. Surrounding the group portrait, my parents proudly displayed large wooden frames with professionally shot baby pictures of me and each of my siblings.

The split-level's kitchen was upstairs, where my mom would cook fufu and spinach stew for my dad, and make Kraft Mac &

Cheese and chicken nuggets for us kids. Next to the kitchen was the dining room, where my little sister's parakeet lived in a cage near the dinner table. Upstairs is where the living room was too. In my family, the "living room" was not actually a room for any of us to live in. It's where the nice furniture lived. We had a long white couch and love seat with pastel flowers on them. Can you imagine? A white couch! In a home with four children! There was no food allowed in the living room, no roughhousing, no lounging around. The living room was where important, serious, seated conversations took place.

Our house was filled with photos, and the side tables overflowed with them. In fading images, my parents are young, hip folks in the 1970s, dressed in bell-bottoms and tightly fitted shirts with sweater vests. They're both short—neither of them over five foot five—but even when my mom is in heels as they strut down the street hand in hand, she always seems to be looking up at my dad. And his eyes genuinely love-gaze back at her.

We had portraits of aunties and uncles and cousins. Photos of us kids playing at the park, a family trip to the zoo. Here we are dressed up in Halloween costumes my mom made for us— three sister witches with green faces and pointy hats, my brother in a Barney costume; me on the split-level's stairs in a bright blue-and-fuchsia polka-dotted clown suit, knees snug to my chest. My dad loved taking pictures, and recently we'd bought a camcorder and begun making family videos to watch back on VHS tapes in the VCR connected to the TV in the basement.

Next to the living room was a pocket door that opened to the hallway. Turn left, and you'd find a bathroom with double sinks and wooden step stools that allowed me and my sisters to crawl up onto the counters and film camcorder videos of ourselves grinning into the big mirror that ran along one wall. Next to the bathroom were two bedrooms: the first was my little brother's room, and at the end of the hall was the guest room, which became Cousin Eman's room after my dad sponsored him to come and live with us in America.

On the opposite end of the hallway, to the right of the pocket door, you'd find a big bedroom—sharing a wall with the living room—which I shared with my two sisters. We had bunk beds. I slept on a twin in the top bunk and my sisters shared a queen on the bottom. My memories of the bedroom, like the house, are split. I felt safe there. Before my baby brother was born, this bedroom was my parents' room—the place I would go to if I was having a nightmare or worried about a monster under the bed. Navy-blue wallpaper with pretty little flowers covered the walls. But sometimes, as we fell asleep in our bunks, we would hear a rustling in those walls. My dad would say it was just squirrels who lived there, but—while she would never tell us as kids—my mom later admitted that she always believed it was bats, not squirrels, who snuck into the walls of our split-level home. Squirrels were just a friendlier intruder to conjure up when trying to put your kids to bed at night.

On this day, I am nine years old and I am sitting on my parents' bed in their room in the basement, watching my father pack a suitcase. He is stacking cans of sardines alongside his clothes and gifts to take back home for his family in Nigeria. He will be away for several weeks. I cannot remember my dad ever having gone away for so long. And I am scared.

Though a bit of a worrywart, I always feel safe. We own this home. We have two cars. We go to public school, and we always have food to eat. My favorites are Fruit Roll-Ups, Gushers, and popcorn with neon-colored butter—hot pink, green, blue, and extra-bright yellow. My mom always cooks dinner: spaghetti in store sauce, baked chicken, mashed potatoes or steamed broccoli covered in Velveeta cheese so us kids will be tricked into eating it. She's the only pediatrician in town, and when she's gone for medical conferences, she leaves food prepped in the fridge for my dad to microwave for us for dinner. Meat loaf or lasagna reheat easily, and a pan lasts for several days while she's away.

When mail comes to the house addressed to Dr. Okokon, my dad jokes and asks, *Which one?* My dad says he's a "doctor of books," which makes me giggle as I imagine him repairing the spines of our *Encyclopaedia Britannica*s. Like my mom, he sometimes goes to conferences for his job too. Once he went to New Orleans and brought me back a pink T-shirt with a carousel on it. As I watch him pack his bags for Nigeria, I try to focus on what he might bring me back from this trip. I don't want to think about how big his suitcases are, or how this means he'll be gone a long time. I don't want to think about how far away Nigeria is, or how I'm worried he might not come back.

Here in River Falls, it seems like everyone knows that my parents are from Africa, like everyone knows our family, and like everyone knows my dad is going away. Most of the kids at school know my mom because she's their doctor. And while I don't know it at the time, some of the teachers—like Ms. Moriarity, whose third-grade class I'm a student in—know my dad from their time as undergrads at the university. My parents are well-respected and well-liked. Friendly and approachable in the way immigrants from the late 1960s often are, they have assimilated as an act of making nice and they are genuinely grateful for the opportunities their new country has afforded them. I don't know any other families where both parents are doctors. I don't know any other families where both parents are African immigrants. In fact, other than my mom's siblings, I do not know *any* other Black families, immigrants or otherwise. River Falls, and my life outside the walls of our home, is almost entirely White.

My dad is going home to pay his respects as his mom has passed away. This is the first time I have heard that term: "passed away." The words, brand-new, are suddenly floating around the split-level, English break-ins to the Ghanaian Fante and Nigerian Pidgin phone calls my parents are having with increased frequency. *Passed away.* It sounds so peaceful, so easy, so smooth and without force. Like when one of my mom's slippery lace doilies falls off a table. Or like an exhale, visible on a cold Wisconsin morning: the way it floats away from me, the way it will slowly disappear before my eyes. *Passed away.* It's such a nice way of saying *died.*

Dad never talks much about his childhood. Do they have carousels there too? Did his mom leave spinach stew and fufu in the fridge for his dad to warm up for dinner when she had to go away for a few days? Did they have a big backyard and neighbors who made them pie every spring? I can't recall asking any of these kinds of questions, and—as a kid—it doesn't seem odd to not know these details of my dad's life. My dad is a grown-up, and grown-ups tell kids things that kids need to know. Both of my parents had lives back Home, and neither of them talks much about those lives. What I know is that everyone in those photos in the living room is family, and that is all I need to know.

My dad has a mustache. He wears his hair in a short, nappy Afro that my mom helps keep groomed with a little electric buzz clipper. He has even brown skin, dark brown eyes, round cheeks, and a smile filled with bright white teeth. He has a beer belly, and across it there is a scar—a smoothed-out space, pink and white in the center, brown and blackened on the edges.

Dad told us he got the scar in a knife fight when defending his sister, but I don't remember him ever saying his sister's name or what the fight was about. And I don't remember him pointing to her—or any of his siblings—in any of the black-and-white photographs that fill the side tables in the living room. This, too, does not seem odd. Why would it? My mom has a bunch of siblings back home in Ghana, and I don't know all of their names either.

Mom also has siblings here in America, but up until Cousin Eman came to live with us, my dad was the only member of his family to have immigrated to America. So while he never talks about them in too much detail, when my dad tumble plays with us or snuggles us in bed—and his belly accidentally exposes itself—he will use the story of his scar to remind us how important family is. We don't know it yet, but the only members of my dad's family we will ever meet are Cousin Eman and my dad's mother.

My dad had always sent money home to help take care of his mother. He loved her. And I know I was supposed to love her too. I was also probably supposed to call her Grandma. But she didn't speak English and their relationship existed in a language I had not been taught to speak, so I'm not sure she would have understood me if I said it anyhow.

She came to visit us just one time, shortly after my baby brother was born. Perhaps I should have questioned why she came for the birth of the first son, and not her prior three granddaughters. I didn't question this, though. My dad always wanted a son, but I didn't think about this from the perspective of him having been raised in a patriarchal society where sons were awarded special benefits—and responsibilities. Elementary-age kids don't have those kinds of thoughts, and besides, I knew that visiting America wasn't easy for my dad's mom to do. It was expensive. Complicated. Grown-up stuff. Back home, my dad's family doesn't have money like we do here in America, so I just accept that it must have been too difficult for his mom to come any sooner.

I was seven when she visited, just two years before she passed away. All of our conversations were verbally one-sided—each of us unable to communicate beyond body language. What look would you make at a granddaughter you'd never met? How would you smile at her? What would you say to her, if you knew she would never understand your words? Unsure of how to look at my dad's mother, what to say, or how to smile, I did so quickly—darting my eyes and the corners of my mouth away in my discomfort. I can't genuinely recall referring to my dad's mom by any name, and I can't say that I loved her in any true or genuine way. It's hard to love someone you don't even know.

But I knew to respect her. I brought her big plastic bowls with soapy water for her to wash her hands. I cleaned up the shards of chicken bones she spat on the floor after sucking the marrow from them at the end of her meals. I answered phone calls from neighbors when she'd gone for a walk, again, and ended up lost, again, wandering around in someone's backyard garden. I went with my mother to bring her back home. I stifled giggles and horror when she responded to my baby brother's cries by attempting to nurse him with her wrinkled breasts. I hugged her. I softened my eyes and smiled when she touched my face and spoke with my dad.

I remember her visit lasting for about a month, but—as an adult—I would learn from my mom and Eman that she visited for six, maybe eight months. I guess that's just how kid-brain works? How memory works? Scenes from my life are condensed or expanded depending on how significant they feel to me now. My dad packing that suitcase with sardines and gifts for his family took maybe thirty minutes? An hour? But for me, the moment lasts forever.

While my dad is away in Nigeria, my mom creates a routine of gathering us near the top of the split-level's stairs, at the family portrait where my dad's white teeth gleam at us every night before bed. She lifts my baby brother into her arms, and he touches our dad's face in the photograph. It started out as soft and gentle. At the beginning of his trip, Dad was calling every night, but days have gone by now, and we haven't heard from him. My brother's good night touches of the photograph have become less and less gentle. More like a nudge. A where-are-you tap tap. An I-need-you jolt.

My mom always says bad news comes—unexpectedly—in the middle of the week. I imagine, then, that it is a Wednesday night while my dad was away, when a bat sneaks into the bedroom I share with my sisters—missing the months-old warning from my dad on the veranda. Still terrified of bats, but now the only adult in the home to fight this intruder, my mom calls the police to help her remove the unwanted houseguest. And I imagine, then, it is the next Wednesday when Uncle Ato enters the arrivals gate that was the split-level's foyer and goes upstairs. We sit with him in the living room. The couch and love seat are so un-lived-on that the white upholstery with sweet pastel florals still clearly shows its colors. The fabric is scratchy and stiff against our skin. Uncle Ato lives far away in Milwaukee, and I can't remember my mom mentioning he was coming to visit.

Sometimes—like this time—when aunties or uncles or friends call or come by, my parents' conversations will all of a sudden change into a language I can no longer follow. Some might find that switch unsettling, or wonder if they're being secretly spoken about. I never do, although: sometimes—like this time—that *is* what's happening.

While my dad didn't teach us Pidgin, I'm told my first word was *aiysch*, which was either Pidgin or just a word my dad made up. When he says *aiysch* it means "shhh," like when he is watching the news. I can imagine myself sitting on the brown short-shag carpet of the basement, watching *20/20* with my dad—half of his attention on me and the other half on the story Barbara Walters is weaving. *Aiysch*, he would say as the show returned from a commercial break. But somehow, when I said the word, I changed its meaning. *Aiysch*, I would say while I reached out, handing my Fruit Roll-Up or yogurt cup to the grown-up or big sister in the room. *Aiysch*, always preceding a plea or directive, but never stated in the form of a question. My family would say that, to me, *Aiysch* meant "open," but as I reflect back now, I see it differently. Aiysch, *I am watching this.* Aiysch, *I cannot hear your mother.* Aiysch, *go to your room.* Or from me: Aiysch, *open this.* Aiysch, *I need you.* I made the command "Be quiet" into "Please help me."

Did you know your body produces a substance similar to morphine when you're in danger? It does it to protect you, to shield you from feeling something you might not be prepared to feel. Perhaps the protective morphine my brain released has muddled my memory of whether or not Uncle Ato looked concerned when he arrived at the split-level that day in 1992. Perhaps it fogged up the details of what we small-talked about on the living room couches that weren't actually meant for the living.

What I remember is my mom and Uncle Ato switching to Fante, and then switching back to English to tell us kids to go to our room. *What's so serious*, I wonder, that the grown-ups need to have a private living room conversation? But just like the Christmas presents in those big black Hefty bags, this directive is no joke. We do as we are told. And like morphine or a protective safety shield, the floral-patterned shared wall between the bedroom and the living room muddles any snatches of their conversation that us kids might otherwise overhear, until my mom walks toward the bedroom and gently opens the door.

Her face is blank. Neither her eyes nor her body give away what she is about to say, and I am too young to know that sometimes—like this time—when my mom is more sad than her body is prepared to feel: She will cut herself off from feeling. Cut herself off from remembering. Go into autopilot, black out, leave her body, and let the morphine in her brain shove her little shell along. It's a skill. An adaptation. I don't know this yet, but I will grow to recognize—and eventually adopt—this expression from my mom. Her hold-it-together face. Her be-strong-for-the-kids posture.

This day, in the middle of this week. This is the moment. This is when I learn my father is dead.

My body takes me downstairs. The only way to get there is to go into the hallway, pass our portraits hanging on the wall, go through the pocket door, and pass the kitchen and the living room. The morphine shoves my nine-year-old shell down the stairs to the split-level's arrivals gate foyer, and down more stairs to the basement. I move past the door under the steps, which opens to a tiny triangular room us kids call "the spider closet" (a place which would have been a better choice than the laundry room for hiding the Christmas presents because we never went in there voluntarily). I pass the fireplace, the redbrick bench, and the iron stand that held the fireplace poker tool. I move toward the couch, brown plaid fabric soft from being lived upon.

This is where I would sit at my father's feet on the short-shag carpet, reaching out for him or anyone else who might help me. This is where we gathered for holidays and birthdays. This is the place we called "the family room."

I turn on the TV to find Eric Clapton's "Tears in Heaven" playing on VH1.

Would you know my name, if I saw you in heaven? Would it be the same, if I saw you in heaven?

Be quiet. Please help me.

Telling a story is how my dad taught a lesson. It's how I learned to remember things. There are huge blank spaces in the stories he told—or didn't tell—us about his life, but I like to think he had a plan to slowly unfurl. Or maybe he *did* tell us more. Maybe I forgot. Maybe I was just a kid and no one said: *Write this down, it's gonna be on the test later.* I didn't know I was supposed to try to remember. I didn't know to ask for more.

Years later, I still feel robbed and resentful for not remembering more of my dad. Instead: I find him in songs he never sang; I tell and retell stories about him, until my mind tricks me into believing I can remember. But the thing about memory is that it shifts. The stories get blurred, lore gets created. My first word becomes *aiysch*, when in reality: it was *Dada*.

When I sat on my parents' bed and watched my dad pack sardines and clothes and gifts to take home to his family, I asked him if he was going to die.

No, he said. *Of course not.*

But no one knows how their story ends, until it's already over.

PART TWO

IT'S OKAY,
YOU DIDN'T KILL HIM

I do not self-identify as the child of a man who was murdered because I cannot say for certain that I am. I cannot say for certain that I'm *not* either. So, immediately following my dad's death, I tended to just not say much of anything at all.

There was an almost-silent hum around the hallways at Westside Elementary School and hushed conversations between the grown-ups when my mom would drop me off for a sleepover at a friend's house. But it seemed like everyone in River Falls had collectively agreed that the details of my dad's death were not up for public discussion—at least not when us kids were around. Years later, I'd come to understand that some of my friends' parents told them he'd been bitten by a poisonous snake, and others heard that he'd fallen to rabies from a bat.

Some questioned if perhaps he'd chosen to leave me, my mom, and my siblings behind. And quietly, the grown-ups began to believe that maybe something more sinister—something retaliatory, perhaps—had happened. But they couldn't say for certain that it was murder. Of course, they couldn't say for certain that it wasn't either.

Whenever anyone asked me what happened to my dad, I took to giving a simple, nonexplanatory response. *He went to Africa for his mom's funeral, and he never came back.* While this didn't seem to lead anyone to assume my dad might have been murdered, it did come across with an unintended air of mystery. And it certainly didn't close the door on any abandonment theories. I spend most of my time uncomfortably avoiding it, but my worst fear is to be abandoned. And my second worst fear is for anyone to *think* I've been abandoned. So, as I got older, I revised my summary response to simply: *My dad died when I was young.*

I learned it was better to remove the mystery. Editing out the "and he never came back" seemed to achieve this, and negating mention that he'd died on a trip to Africa somehow softened the abandonment and shame I felt in my dad leaving us behind. Only fellow members of the Dead-Dad Club would interpret dying as a form of leaving—and they would be too busy dealing with their own versions of self-inflicted shame to ask me any further questions.

My dad died when I was young, I'd say. And everyone else would hear it, be sad, and then find a way to quickly move the conversation forward, lest my Dead-Dad cooties rub off on them.

Oh, I'm so sorry, they'd say. Accidentally (or on purpose) making the moment about their feelings, not mine. *It's okay*, I'd say. On purpose. Because any good member of the Dead-Dad Club knows that it is our job to salve your sadness.

As a kid (and TBH still now), the only way I could watch a scary movie was by convincing myself that the plot could never happen to me. I didn't tell ghost stories. I'd never puked up something that looked like pea soup. I hadn't done anything last summer. As long as I couldn't *imagine* the scary thing happening to me, it couldn't happen. I think sometimes that's why people don't ask what happened to my dad. It's easier when you can't imagine it happening to you too.

But as I grew up, I got tired of silently being asked to hold everyone else's fear, sadness, or discomfort. So eventually, I made another revision to my response.

Oh, I'm so sorry, they'd say.

It's okay, I'd respond. *You didn't kill him.*

It made people uncomfortable to receive this reply: And that was the point. My existence had become rooted in my own discomfort, and I was happy to spread those cooties to anyone who even inched toward getting too close. The details of my dad's death continued to be shrouded in a hushed silence, but the theory that his family might have been involved was becoming increasingly prevalent. Although that was not a story I was open to telling. Not yet, at least.

Instead, conversations about my dad's death would continue as I had scripted them to:

My dad died when I was young.

Oh, I'm so sorry.

It's okay. You didn't kill him.

I said it all the time because it was true. Until it wasn't.

• • •

I BET we're cousins! Alyssa exclaimed in our first conversation. *I'm going to ask my dad if he knows your dad!*

Outside of my immediate family, Alyssa Okokon is the only Okokon I have ever connected with. I found her on Facebook, and our entire relationship existed over instant messages. I'd just graduated from college and was still living in Green Bay, and she was living somewhere in the south: Alabama or Tennessee. Since our last name—which means "night-night"—is rare, we were both surprised to find another Okokon living in America.

Alyssa and I exchanged stories about our lives and where we were raised. She was so bubbly, so enthusiastic to connect with me. I was excited and hopeful, but there was a part of me who knew better. I found myself holding back, knowing somewhere deep down that our relationship was unlikely to last. I told her my dad had passed away years before, but I didn't tell her how. It still wasn't a story I was open to telling, nor even one I'd allowed myself to fully believe. Not yet.

Oh, I am so sorry, she said.

It's okay, I wrote back.

I imagine my fingertips pausing over the QWERTY of my keyboard. Typing the characters to spell *you didn't kill him* as a follow-up, and then deleting them. I obviously didn't think *Alyssa* had killed my dad, and it was hard for me to imagine that she knew who had. But sometimes the truth is unimaginable. I had begun to accept the theories that my dad's death may have happened at the hands—or under the watch—of someone he called family. So while I knew Alyssa hadn't killed my dad, by then I knew it was entirely possible that someone *she* called family had.

My dad says we might be cousins, Alyssa wrote after a week of near silence, an implied shrug and shift in the tone of her Facebook instant message. And then she never came back. I never heard from her again.

It's been over a decade, and I still regularly search my Messenger history for the word "cousins," hoping to reread our old messages. But they've vanished. This can probably be easily explained by Alyssa having deactivated her account, but I constantly question my memory of her. Was she real? Did our conversations actually happen? If there's no evidence, how can I prove it?

Every once in a while I'll search Facebook for people who share my last name, seeking anyone hidden in the plain sight of night-night all around the world, but mostly in Nigeria. In a recent search, I found an account for a guy who looked like Cousin Eman. His profile said he lived near my dad's village, and his eyes stared plainly through his camera and into my bedroom. To

I scrolled through this man's friends list of names similar to mine, my siblings', my dad's. I returned to his image—his face friendly and familiar—and felt my heart start to race.

Was it you? Do you know? Were you in on it?

I've never done one of those mail-away DNA tests, and I don't like to imagine what might happen if I did. Being abandoned may be my greatest fear, but getting connected could be even worse.

THE DAYBED

A year after my dad's death, my mom moved our now family of five across the state to Mequon, Wisconsin, the Milwaukee suburb where she originally lived after immigrating. Our new house was modest by Mequon standards: five bedrooms, two and a half baths, no high-tech upgrades, and an unfinished basement. As the eldest, Veronica had a room of her own now, as did our little brother—although since Dad died, he'd started sleeping on the floor of Mom's room.

I'd been saddled with sharing a bedroom with Affi. It was a big room, plenty of space for two preteens, and we'd been allowed to decorate it ourselves. We picked matching bedspreads, mine a muted sea-foam green with white polka dots, hers in the same pattern with a pastel-blue background. A wallpaper border matching the polka-dotted motif crowned each wall, and two metal desks—one light green and one light blue—sat at the foot of each of our daybeds.

It was a beautiful room, but it didn't matter to preteen me that I'd gotten to decorate the space a shade of my favorite color, because I wasn't interested in sharing a room with my kid sister. She was lame and wanted to put N*SYNC posters on the wall, while I was a cool kid—trying to memorize the lyrics to No Doubt's "Just a Girl."

Since a handful of our aunties, uncles, and cousins lived in the Milwaukee area, we went from being the relatives others might road-trip to visit over summer vacation to being one of the many family homes where the Memorial Day barbecue might take place that year. Cousin Eman stayed in River Falls for college, and would come to visit us in the new house maybe twice a year. But other than that, our new guest bedroom— along with its double closet, window seat, and bright yellow sink—was going largely unused. I desperately wanted a space of my own, and after about a year, my pleas for my mom to allow this turned into outright demands.

Eman doesn't live with us anymore! I would scream at her. *It's stupid to keep the room open just for him!*

We'd left River Falls on a summer day when other families were heading out for road trips or vacation, and as we cruised along the highway, my friend Allison's minivan came sauntering up in the next lane over. Allison and I waved furiously at each other. We giggled and stuck out our tongues and dramatically pressed our palms to the windows. *Stop! Stop!* I commanded my mother. *We must have left something behind and she's trying to tell us!*

Theresa, they're just living their lives and happen to be driving in the same direction, my mom responded plainly. *They're not trying to tell us anything, and they're not coming with us.*

I was going into fifth grade, and it felt like everything had changed. My dad was gone, and he was never coming back. I was leaving behind every friend I'd ever had, and now I was the new kid with no anchor. Back in River Falls, I'd never had any trouble making friends, so throughout fifth grade in Mequon I kept holding out hope that I would find my crew, eventually. I imagined hosting sleepovers with a group of girlfriends, staying up late to prank call our crushes and giggling when our MASH games declared we would get married to Jonathan Taylor Thomas, live in a mansion, and have seventeen children with him. I simultaneously wanted to be embraced by someone—anyone—and wanted to be left alone. In a room of my own. And my sights were set on the almost-always-empty guest bedroom.

What if someone in the family needs a place to stay? my mom would remind me. *That room is for them.*

Whenever my parents spoke of family, they didn't just mean blood relatives. They meant Uncle Martin, one of my dad's friends from back Home who lived with us before my parents bought the split-level. They meant Auntie Marie, my god-mother and my mom's best friend from medical school. And now in the new house in Mequon, my mom wanted to keep the guest room open for just about anyone who might show up at one of those Memorial Day barbecues.

But I really didn't care. We'd been in Mequon for almost a year, and it sure didn't seem like anyone was coming to be with us. It seemed to me like everyone else was just living their own lives, and I was intent to live mine as I saw fit.

One day, I mustered up all of my preteen angst and tore my polka-dotted comforter off my daybed. I ripped out the matching bed skirt, propped the mattress up against the wall, and pushed the bed frame through my shared bedroom door. I kept pushing the daybed through the double doors that led into the computer room, and then down another hall toward the guest room. Through sheer force of will, I managed to get the daybed halfway through the guest room door until it would not budge any farther.

My mom refused to help me. *You can sleep right there in that doorway if you want, but you're not getting your own bedroom.*

I called her bluff. I went back for my mattress, hoisted it over the hallway edge of the wooden bed frame, and plopped it onto the daybed's mattress springs. I billowed my polka-dotted comforter and watched it fall over the mattress, then went back and grabbed my tchotchkes—troll dolls, art-class ceramics projects, the Elmo doll I'd purchased in an adolescent effort toward nostalgia and irony. I hung my clothes in the double closet, plugged in my boom box, and arranged my toothbrush and a brand-new tube of toothpaste next to the yellow sink. I had transported my life over the daybed bridge, and this was my room now.

I happily slept in that doorway for days before my mom finally relented.

Eventually, everyone accepted that the guest room was Theresa's room now. My mom hired our neighbor, an interior decorator, to help me transform the space into the bedroom of my teenage dreams. We painted the walls jewel-toned purple, blue, and green, and I picked out butterfly-print bedsheets and a rainbow-striped comforter from dELiA*s. When I got a job at The Exclusive Company, a local CD store, I would bring home posters of my favorite musicians—Ani, Alanis, Fiona, Madonna—and plaster my walls with their images.

Eventually, I would make friends and have those sleepovers I'd been dreaming of. And whenever my friends came over, we could hang out in *my* room with *my* stuff, listening to *my* music, and have no annoying kid sister to pester us. One year I convinced my mom I needed Wite-Out pens during our annual school-supplies shopping trip, and then I used the pens to have my friends sign their names to the daybed's wooden frame, like a giant yearbook, further decorated with glittery butterfly stickers and a rub-on decal declaring myself a "Bitch Goddess."

I was becoming who I wanted to be, and I was quick to pretend that I was doing it all by myself and on my own terms.

WHITE KIDS

B ack in River Falls, we were the only Black family at school. And since school is an elementary kid's universe: for me that meant we were the only Black family in town, period. It never seemed like anyone had any expectations for how we— as Black people—were supposed to present ourselves. Black girls did their hair the way my sisters and I did ours. Black kids listened to the music we listened to. Black kids dressed like us, danced like us, behaved like us.

At our house, we watched *The Fresh Prince of Bel-Air* on Mondays, and *Family Matters* with TGIF. We weren't rich like the Banks family, but we weren't too far off from the Winslows. So even within the expanded galaxy of our tube television, I was just like everyone else.

I mean, sure, I'd seen *Yo! MTV Raps*, so I knew that not all Black people were like my family. But I figured maybe there were formal categories. Maybe "Black people" were like the folks on MTV, and maybe *we* were "African Americans." At the age of ten or eleven, racial dynamics were not at the top of my radar; in fact they didn't even register on the list of things I was aware of, cared about, or committed any thought to at all. We were Black, and in River Falls there was no mold for us to fill. We were the prototype.

When we moved across the state, this reality quite suddenly shifted. On the one hand: More than 60 percent of the Black people in the state of Wisconsin live in the city of Milwaukee; so to put it plainly: we moved to where the Black people were. On the other hand: we lived in the suburb of Mequon, which—like all of Milwaukee's northern suburbs—is overwhelmingly White.

The Mequon-Thiensville School District had three elementary schools, two middle schools, and one high school. The entire district participated in an initiative unaffectionately referred to as the 220 program, named for the state legislature's decades-old Chapter 220, aimed at desegregating schools. There were no Black boys in my grade at Donges Bay Elementary, but there were a handful of other Black girls. I became the second Black girl in my grade who lived within the city of Mequon; everyone else was bussed in with the 220 program. While this was my first experience having Black classmates, I wouldn't have thought it was a big deal that the other Black girls leaned toward the *Yo! MTV Raps* side of the spectrum. But they seemed to regard me as a foreigner.

It was fifth grade: the last year of elementary school, when everyone seems to have their friendship groups clearly defined. I was not only the new kid at school; I was the new *Black* kid. To put it plainly: the mold had been set and it was now my job to fill it.

At recess, the White kids played four square and swung around on the elaborate playground equipment, courtesy of the well-funded tax revenue from my new, wealthy, suburban school district. My instinct was to race for an optimal spot in line to traverse the jungle gym, but all the other Black girls gathered on the concrete to jump Double Dutch. They would laugh as I stood frozen and mesmerized by the swinging Double Dutch ropes, absolutely unable to jump in. None of the White kids at Donges Bay jumped Double Dutch at recess; this was a Black girls thing. And *all* the Black girls at Donges Bay could Double Dutch. Except me.

Recess wasn't the only thing I was seemingly incapable of getting right either. From day one, the other Black girls cracked what felt like endless jokes about how I talked "too proper" and how my jeans were too tight. But it didn't feel like joking to me at the time. I'm sure the White kids held expectations for us, too, but on the playground of fifth grade: It was the Black girls I wanted to fit in with. There couldn't have been more than five or six of us total, and all I wanted was for them to like me, to see me as one of them, to consider me their friend.

I tried to watch *Martin* and *Living Single* so that I could join in on their lunchroom conversations, but when I held the reins over our family room remote control, I more naturally gravitated toward *Full House* and reruns of *The Brady Bunch*. I tried to remember to switch the dial to V100 so I could memorize the lyrics to Aaliyah songs, but alone in my bedroom I was hitting record on my tape deck whenever Casey Kasem's Top 40 played Lisa Loeb's "Stay," then whirring it to rewind until the tape scrambled or I knew every word—whichever came first.

When I checked my reflection in the mirror at Kohl's department stores, baggy jeans never seemed to sit on my hips in a way that I could rock outside the confines of a private fitting room. Instead, I bought an oversized T-shirt with Bugs Bunny,

Sylvester, and Tweety Bird dressed in baggy jeans and backward caps and I wore it to school as much as the house laundry rotation would allow. It never would have occurred to me to interrogate the ways in which this shirt depicted caricatures of Blackness—literal cartoons—that did nothing but perpetuate the very stereotypes that made my daily life so immensely uncomfortable. I did not care and was not thinking about that. Instead, I pulled my Bugs Bunny shirt over my tapered jeans and hoped for the best.

It should come as no surprise that my Looney Tunes meets *Yo! MTV Raps* T-shirt did absolutely nothing to build my cachet with the other Black girls at school. But as we entered sixth grade, the handful of Black kids in my grade became even more diluted in the now slightly larger pool of the student body at Lake Shore Middle School. With more new-friend options, I decided to branch out and see where else I might be able to fit in.

Trying to be Black wasn't working, and before moving to Mequon, I didn't even have any conscious thoughts about *wanting* to be Black—I just *was* Black. My teachers continued to spoon-feed us the 1990s whitewashed ideals of America being a great melting pot, and I eagerly slurped it up. Eventually, I stopped *trying* to be Black, and at some point: I stopped thinking of myself as having any race at all. I just wanted to be like everyone else. The trouble was that once the Black girls rejected me, "everyone else" in Mequon was White.

At Lake Shore Middle School, I was less and less concerned with willing my limbs to jump Double Dutch at recess, and directed my focus instead on finding a crew who might accept me as cool, fun to be around, and just like them. My homeroom teacher looked like Santa Claus and began every day by playing the Bee Gees' "Stayin' Alive" from a battered boom box behind his desk. I thought he was a weird dude, but I was never so grateful as when he assigned me a seat next to a blond, freckle-faced girl named Bianca.

Bianca not only had friends in our homeroom but she seemed to know at least one kid in every sixth grade classroom. The first time our Santa Claus teacher paired us up to complete an in-class worksheet together, I prepared myself to apologize to Bianca's groans, rolled eyes, or extended fingers to her bestie like they were being ripped apart at the seams—but she never did that. Instead, Bianca smiled, introduced herself, and tugged my desk closer to hers. Just like that, Bianca and I were friends, and within weeks, her friends were my friends too.

We wore short shorts with frayed edges, baby-doll tops, and

Keds. We hung out at Northridge Mall, shopped at dELiA*s, PacSun, and the Gap, and had crushes on skater boys. Bianca would scrunch her nose and plug her ears whenever I turned up the volume on the Cranberries' "Zombie," but for my birthday she got me the cassette of *No Need to Argue*—along with a card that said I had to promise to not play the song one more time in her presence. I'd gone from being the mostly lonely new kid in a new school in a new town in fifth grade to finally finding my niche in sixth grade. I had friends who thought I was cool— even if I wasn't exactly the same as them—and I was prepared to do whatever it took to stay in their good graces. Shaving my legs seemed to be the upcoming price of admission.

Shaving only makes it so there's more hair! my mom insisted. But I did not care and was not tryna hear all that. As the last day of sixth grade approached, Bianca had extended to me the invitation I'd been waiting for: to hang out with her at the OCC. The Ozaukee Country Club is a members-and-their-guests-only golf club with a glimmering swimming pool set back behind iron gates and manicured shrubbery. Several of my classmates were members, but I'd never been invited to go. Until now.

The OCC opened in 1922, during the era of legal segregation, and I have to imagine its founders followed (if not personally believed in the virtue of) the law of the land at the time. Of course, as a rising seventh grader, I was not thinking about when Black people like me would have first been allowed to visit the OCC. *My* life was happening *now*. And even if I was only a temporary guest, I had still been invited in. That was all I cared about.

The OCC's golf course butted right up against the house where Bianca's family lived, a house that was—in my middle school eyes—a mansion. Her front door opened to a grand staircase, and the wall-to-wall carpeting was the same in every room. I'm pretty sure there was even a remote control for the fireplace, plus a three-car garage with a convertible inside. A white cement driveway. A whirlpool tub. And more bathrooms than family members. Lots of the families in Mequon were more on the Banks-family side of the spectrum than the Winslow side, so Bianca's family hardly seemed unique or unusual by those standards. Their very obvious wealth was not what lured me. I was drawn to Bianca quite simply because she was kind to me. She liked me. She was easy to be around, and she didn't make me feel like I should question who I was. That was enough.

Still: Bianca's life was—undeniably—fancy. And she was already shaving, so there was no way that I was going to show up at the OCC with hair on my legs. Sure, I was wearing short shorts to school: so anyone who cared to look would have already noticed my hairy legs in the halls of Lake Shore Middle School for the entirety of sixth grade, when it started to grow in. But I did not care and was not thinking about that. My big sis had ventured into Nair hair-removal territory by then, stinking up the entire upstairs of our house with noxious fumes every couple of weeks. I didn't quite want to go to that extreme, but I had started begging my mom to let me shave my legs.

When she finally relented, Mom took me to a drugstore and helped me pick out my first pack of pink plastic razors with flowers embossed on the handle and a can of puffy, floral-scented Skintimate shaving cream. She didn't give me much direction on what to do next, so as soon as we got home, I locked myself in the bathroom and tried to recollect the *Brady Bunch* scene where the dad teaches the oldest brother to shave his sprouting beard. An hour or so later, I emerged a new woman. I was as bare as I could muster, with bits of toilet paper collecting blood in spots where I'd nicked myself—just like the Brady dad had taught Greg.

I'm sure there was some boy I was hoping would see my hairless legs as I reclined on a poolside beach chair at the OCC, coyly munching hot dogs and licking ice cream cones on Bianca's family's tab. I imagine the boy I was hoping to see that day was Adam, a cute, Catholic-school kid with green eyes and sandy-blond hair, on whom I had an absolutely raging crush. We would smile meekly at each other when our schools' shared buses stopped at Lake Shore Middle School at the end of the day, and all of my friends knew I had a crush on Adam. I'm sure I wasn't subtle about it—squeezing my pinkie and ring fingers tightly as I wished for Adam to be the boy my MASH game would declare I would marry, and drawing his name in bubble letters surrounded by hearts in the margins of my notebooks. Just as many MASH games predicted, Adam *did* become my boyfriend eventually (sometime after rumors spread about him getting caught masturbating in the Catholic-school bathroom), but for now: my crush raged on.

I assumed Adam was a member of the OCC because it was a rich people thing, and he went to *private* school so I mean ... he was rich, right? My crush wasn't rooted in his presumed richness—because similar to how I perceived Bianca's family at the time, wealth was a thing I noticed, but not something I really cared about. And truthfully, beyond the undeniable fact of his cuteness, I knew next to nothing at all about the kid, really. I didn't need to know much about a boy to have a crush on him. Adam was cute and he smiled back at me. That was enough.

I also wouldn't have cared or even been thinking about how I was likely to be the only Black person at the OCC that day. Even with the 220 program, I was used to being the only Black person in any given classroom, and I have literally never in my life had a Black teacher. This stark lack of representation wouldn't occur to me until decades later, when I realized that "representation" was even a thing. And that summer at the OCC, it hadn't started to hit me that I'd likely become the only person who paid no mind to how much I stood out. My friends told me I was just like them, and—blinded by my melting-pot-tinted glasses—I believed it. So if Adam were to put his hand on my naked, smooth-skinned, brown calf and remark about how I "didn't even need to get tanned," I'd have considered myself lucky to have my dream boy notice me.

A year later, the summer between seventh and eighth grade, was the 1996 Olympic Games, featuring the Magnificent Seven women's gymnastics team. My sisters and I would pedal our bikes down to our subdivision's pool (which was, admittedly, also for members and their guests only) and poise ourselves to swan dive into the deep end. We would conjure up the gymnastics team, trying to mimic their graceful poses.

Among the Magnificent Seven there were two Dominiques: Dawes and Moceanu. I'm sure the Olympics announcers referred to them by their names—or maybe just as Dominique D and Dominique M—but in my head: they were Black Dominique and White Dominique. And despite having never heard the word "representation," I was beginning to have a nagging thought in the back of my mind that when I prepared for my swan dives, it was wrong of me to imagine myself as White Dominique—not Black Dominique, the only Black girl on the team.

It's not that I didn't *know* I was Black; it's just that no one really talked about it. In the nineties, no one was discussing race the way we do today, especially not middle and high school kids. The unspoken mentality was that the mere acknowledgment of race was racist. So when White Dominique came to mind as I mounted the diving board, I wasn't squeezing my eyes shut and interrogating my internalized anti-Blackness. Whether I was trying to make baggy jeans work, trying to jump Double Dutch, shaving my legs, or pretending I was an Olympic gymnast as I dove into the pool: like most adolescents, I was constantly trying to be someone other than who I was.

The truth is, Black Dominique's bangs looked like mine did whenever I burned myself while trying a little too hard to get the perfect bump from my curling iron. While White Dominique, on the other hand, looked like the kind of girl who the boys I had crushes on would crush on back—even before they ran out of options after everyone had found out they'd been caught masturbating in the bathroom at Catholic school. And by this time, having boys like me was just as important as having the girls like me.

By eighth grade, my general desire to fit in had transformed into a silent campaign to amass as many friends as possible: and I was at the top of my game. I was voted student council vice president. I got the second-highest number of one-dollar Valentine's Day carnations from my classmates, my friends, and a few secret admirers. Everyone was happy to sign the back pages of my yearbook, and friends like Bianca made sure my locker was always decorated for my birthday. Any mimicry from the other Black girls at school had either dissipated or faded to the background of my consciousness. I'd become who I wanted to be, and I felt accepted for who I was.

The inside of my locker was plastered with pictures of boys

carefully torn out of *Teen*, *Seventeen*, and *YM*. Jared Leto with his intentionally greasy brown hair and piercing blue eyes. Luke Perry and his angled jaw, a bad boy with do-good sensibilities. And Leonardo DiCaprio, perma-sweaty and in love from *Romeo + Juliet*. White boys with bowl cuts and center parts were my thing. And just like all the boys in my locker, almost all of my crushes at school were White. Should I have seen that as a problem to ponder? Why? What more was there to think about it? White boys sent me carnations. They signed my yearbook. They fished pens from their Trapper Keepers to wish me happy birthday by signing the placard on my wrapped locker each year. Besides, despite the larger pool of boys in my grade to have crushes on at Lake Shore Middle School, White boys were still the majority option. So, White boys were who I liked—even after it slowly became obvious that they had stopped liking me back.

I had a smattering of boyfriends going into the beginning of ninth grade at Homestead High School. I might have to ask more than one, but eventually some boy would say yes when I invited him to the Sadie Hawkins dance, and eventually some boy would ask me to homecoming (although I never seemed to be anyone's first-round pick). My crushes continued, and I

WHO I ALWAYS WAS

was still scribbling their names with hearts in the margins of my notebooks, and composing ridiculous songs about them that I would sing to myself in the shower. But just like crushes, dance dates, and the month when Catholic schoolboy Adam became my boyfriend after never showing up that day at Bianca's OCC pool: the White boys in Mequon liking me back would prove to be temporary. By ninth grade, it became clear that these boys were never going to see me the way I longed for them to. Because whether or not I or anyone else acknowledged it aloud, my skin wasn't just a tan. I could straighten my hair and carefully curl my bangs every morning—but that didn't change who I was. I might dress like the White girls, talk like the White girls, and listen to the same kind of music that all the White kids listened to, but I wasn't *really* one of them.

I cannot imagine that my teenage classmates were thinking about the possibility of spending their lives partnered with the girl they invited to walk hand in hand with around Northridge Mall on a Saturday afternoon. But it is impossible for forty-something-year-old me to believe race played zero role in the boys at my high school not wanting to date me. Still, I struggle with what to call that. Racism? Misogynoir? I can't say that any of this was consciously present for any of my classmates any more than it was for me. But was it for their parents? Did they covertly discuss it in front of their remote-control fireplaces? Were they able to push past their midwestern politeness and find the words to subtly articulate their ideals about who they wanted their kids to date?

Let's pretend for a moment that the library at Homestead High School held books about race theory. Let's imagine it was even possible for me—a 1990s teenager—to have had the capacity to interrogate the complicated dynamics playing out in my everyday suburban Wisconsin life. Had I allowed myself to recognize what was going on, it would have only served to cause me pain. The not caring, not thinking, not noticing: it was all a balm against the millions of potential paper cuts from the microaggressions—self-inflicted and otherwise—that I was swimming in. Because while I can confidently say that I was not aware of any of it, I am not foolish enough to presume this verbal violence was absent from the dinner table in the homes and country clubs of my classmates and temporary boyfriends.

As a high schooler, I was cute, petite, smart, artsy, and on Fridays, I wore my pleated polyester dance team skirt and a simple tank top: the team's way of making sure everyone knew there was a game that night. But by tenth grade, the boys—

including Homestead's small handful of Black and otherwise not-White boys—either were not interested in me or inexplicably always had a crush on one of my White girlfriends. So, high school Theresa started going out with White boys from other schools, and since these boys were all older than I was: I told myself it was because I was cool, desirable, mature.

My new crushes were White boys who wore gold chains, drove fast cars, and listened to rap music booming from custom speakers. White boys who plastered the walls of their bedrooms with the covers of *XXL* and *The Source*. Ghetto Whiteboys—my friends and I called them—who were merely attempting a caricature of Blackness, not at all dissimilar to my Looney Tunes T-shirt. And consciously or not, their desire to date me was likely related to their fetishization of Black women or their desire to create proximity to a culture they coveted.

None of that occurred to me at the time, and even if it had: I wouldn't have cared. I fit the mold that they wanted, and they fit the mold I wanted to fit into. As much as they were fetishizing me, I, too, was coveting proximity to whatever scraps of pseudo-Blackness and acceptance the ghetto Whiteboys could offer. They did it to me, and I was doing it right back to them and all the other White kids I grew up with.

MY FIRST KISS
WAS A GAME

1999

When I was sixteen I went to a New Year's Eve party and a ghetto Whiteboy named Blake wrote his number on a torn-off piece of a brown paper bag, shoved it into his pocket, and then proceeded to ignore me for the entire evening. As my hand reached the doorknob to leave that night, Blake tapped my shoulder and said, *If I gave you my number, would you call me?* I nodded, which we both fairly presumed meant yes. But I never actually uttered my response out loud.

I'd spotted Blake as soon as I set foot into that New Year's Eve party, and while I was immediately attracted to his over-sized jeans, freshly ironed Ecko shirt, and pristinely clean K-Swiss shoes, I never even tried to say so much as a single word to him all night. Instead, I spent the evening communicating my attraction by creating proximity while feigning disinterest. The first time we actually had a conversation was when I followed Blake's directive and called him at the number he'd given me.

We spoke briefly, and Blake asked if he could take me out to the movies. I'd only ever been on one real date before, and my mom had driven me to and from that one in our Toyota minivan—so I eagerly and enthusiastically accepted Blake's invitation to pick me up. We agreed to seeing *The World Is Not Enough*—the latest James Bond movie—for our first date. And by "agreed" I mean: Blake suggested it, and I said yes. I'm sure I was more interested in seeing *Girl, Interrupted* or *Magnolia*, but those were chick flicks. Any quizzes I'd taken or articles I'd read in *Marie Claire* or *Cosmo* had made it clear that relationships were about compromise. So, sure, I was more interested in a movie about women's mental health or one set to an entire soundtrack of Aimee Mann songs, but a title track from Garbage would have to suffice.

A few days later, Blake held my hand as we sat silently in the theater. I can't recall him ever asking or my ever confirming: but Blake became my boyfriend that night. I imagine that we pulled up to my house, and he allowed his old-school, light-blue Chevy

Caprice to idle next to my little brother's skateboarding ramp in the driveway. He would have leaned across the front seat to kiss me and then asked me to be his girlfriend. I would have said yes, giggled, and then raced inside to log into AOL and tell all my friends. Blake was neither my first date nor my first kiss, but he became my first of many things. He was my first love. My first blow job, the first person to go down on me, the first person I would have sex with, and the first boy who made me cry.

Within a few months of that Chevy Caprice first-date movie night, my friend walked in on Blake putting his penis inside of another girl's mouth. I confronted him about it, he denied and then finally admitted it, and I sobbed. I wish I could say that I heard myself crying that night. Heard my pain, knew I deserved better, pulled myself together, walked away, and never looked back. But that's not what happened.

Instead, I would define the end of my teens and the beginning of my twenties around being Blake's girlfriend. I would follow him to Green Bay for college, and his electric-blue Honda Civic (which he upgraded to a year or so into our relationship) would become an illegally parked staple in the cul-de-sac outside my freshman-year dorm. I would put on sweats when Blake was coming over, but my sophomore-year roommates would do their hair and makeup and casually prance around our apartment in baby-doll tops and short shorts when they knew he would be visiting. Blake was the kind of guy who lots of girls wanted to be with. He hung out with the basketball players and the kids who sold weed, he went to clubs every weekend, and the boom of the base from his Civic's custom speakers could be heard from a solid mile away.

Have you ever lived in an old house where the floors squeak? You get so used to which spots will creak under the weight of even your lightest footsteps that if one day you were to tiptoe across the threshold and be confronted with silence, you would be surprised. That was Blake. My squeaky floorboard. My old house with a sinking foundation that I convinced myself was comfortable. Underage and without a fake ID, I told myself that I was happy to be the girl who Blake came home to. I told myself that this was the girl I wanted to be.

Blake would spend four and a half years hiding my toothbrush and curling iron under his kitchen sink, shoving the lingerie he bought me between his box spring and mattress, and insisting to me that the box of condoms I bought to keep at his off-campus apartment was empty because he had "masturbated into them." And I would spend four and a half years pretending to believe him. I was the girl Blake was cheating on, and everybody—including me—knew it.

Blake cannot be blamed for who I was, who I became, or who I've become—honestly, he doesn't deserve that much credit. By the time I met him at that New Year's Eve party, by the time I silently accepted the way he treated me, by the time I allowed myself to believe that half the lyrics from Ani DiFranco's "Little Plastic Castle" were actually about us: I was already well steeped in the tea of 1990s and early 2000s toxic tropes of femininity.

I learned about sex from watching *The Montel Williams Show* as a latchkey kid after school, but beyond rom-coms, sitcoms, or those teen-magazine quizzes: I cannot tell you exactly where or when or *how* I—or any adolescent girl coming of age in the nineties—came to believe that interest, acceptance, and even consent was communicated with silence. What I know is that by the time I was sixteen and Blake came along, those lessons were already deeply ingrained within me.

1994

As a rising sixth, seventh, and eighth grader, I attended College Camp at the University of Wisconsin–River Falls, where my father was once a professor. College Camp was for kids of color across the state who got good grades during the school year. And outside of it being a space where White people weren't the majority (or even present at all), College Camp was nothing like what my school friends would describe as their summertime camp experiences. Instead of canoeing or archery in idyllic pastures, we attended "fun" science and "fun" math classes in college classrooms. In the evenings, we didn't gather around campfires and sing songs while toasting s'mores and telling ghost stories. We gathered in the common areas of the dormitories on campus, our lodging for the summer. These rooms were almost always in a basement, half windows near the tops of the walls, a heavy musky-dusty smell weighing in the air.

One night in my first summer at College Camp, a group of us gathered in the common area to play a game. It was similar to Suck and Blow—like they play in that house-party scene in *Clueless* (*Gawd, Elton, can't you suck?!*). Except this was a bit before that movie would come out and long before its lasting impact on my adolescent behavior (and my fashion sense well into adulthood) would become undeniable. Some of the older kids seemed to know the rules, but as a rising sixth grader I had no idea what we were doing. I shuffled silently in my Keds, looking from side to side, trying to appear calm and cool while avoiding making eye contact with anybody.

Playing into the unquestioned cisgender binaries and presumed straightness of the nineties, we lined up boy, girl, boy, girl. We didn't have a credit card (be that a cardboard prop, or otherwise) like Cher, Tai, and Elton did—we had a blown-up wad of Bazooka bubble gum, pink and wet. The first kid would mash on the gum for a bit, softening the hard exterior with his saliva and the strength of his molars, before sealing off the bubble with his front teeth. He passed the bubble to the girl next to him, she passed it to the next boy, he the next girl, and so on. Eventually, the bubble would pop, and whichever couple's mouths were holding the lukewarm pink potato had to kiss.

The Bazooka went from one set of lips to the next, and I held my breath in an attempt to quiet my excitement as I watched the bubble finally get to Jared. He was light-skinned, lanky, quiet, and kind, and as Jared passed the Bazooka to me, someone let out an *OoooOoo* sound. Because everyone at College Camp knew that Jared and I were going out.

By "going out" I do not mean that Jared and I ever actually went anywhere. Rather, it signified that Jared had openly declared that he liked me, and in response I had giggled, my cheeks had flared but didn't flush (a benefit of brown skin), and in front of everyone, Jared became my boyfriend. I'm sure he posed his invitation as a question, but I don't believe I ever actually said yes. I suppose—supposed—I didn't need to. On both ends of this teeter-totter of early understanding, Jared and I casually communicated consent with silence.

Our courting process had involved several days of silent communication, all over campus. In an elevator on the way to science class, Jared would get in after me, stand in front of me, and face the door (as one does). I would wonder if his heart had leapt the same way mine had when our eyes briefly met, but I wouldn't say hello or attempt to chitchat. Instead, I'd stand there studying the back of his body, molding my body to hold its shape just like his, and hoping he might feel my mimicked presence behind him.

Jared would shift his weight to the right, and I'd shift mine. Jared would put his hand in his pocket, and I would mine. As Jared scratched his head, I would pause. The elevator would beep from one floor to another as I casually glanced around, wondering if anyone else was noticing how much Jared and I had in common, just before my hand would reach to scratch my not-itching scalp.

Pop it, Jared. Kiss her! one of the boys in Suck and Blow urged. Jared turned to me (and I turned to him). I didn't need to wait for his eyes to tell mine what to do; we both followed our social and simultaneous instincts to avoid looking at each other. The soft, wet, pink bubble fizzled between our lips. Perhaps on purpose. Perhaps just weighed down by the saliva and expectations of everyone else in the room. We went to the kitchenette area for privacy, and I had my first kiss in a place where generations of college students would learn to make sodium-rich, quick noodle dishes like Top Ramen and Easy Mac. My mind goes blank when I try to remember the kiss itself, but I imagine it, too, tasted salty-sweet.

In the intervening decades, I have often found myself wondering if this was Jared's first kiss too. I wonder which magazines and movies preteen-Jared consumed that taught him how to interact with preteen-me. I wonder if he wishes any part of that moment in the kitchenette had gone differently. I wonder if the moment mattered to him the way it did to me, if he even remembers it at all.

Most of all, I wonder if this is a story Jared tells about his life. I want it to be. Jared and I are Facebook friends, but I'm far too embarrassed to ask. Too worried he's forgotten, his memory weighed down with the saliva of every moment and kiss that has followed.

1996

The playground at Lake Shore Middle School had no swings and no slides. It was just an extension of the parking lot, with a few painted-on four-square grids, a hopscotch, and a giant, multicolored map of the United States. I guess the district had decided that middle schoolers didn't need monkey bars or grass anymore.

Along the parking lot's perimeter, just to the left of the school's big cement front steps, was a sidewalk with benches. During every recess of seventh grade, I'd kill time with a few games of four square while I waited for Eric Aronson to take his seat on the bench. Then I'd casually let my body gravitate toward him and sit on his lap.

If either of us spoke, it was to those around us and not to each other. Eric Aronson would tip his hips backward and forward, grinding his crotch into my butt. I'd reach my hands behind me to grab hold of his thigh, coyly and dangerously close to his dick. Sometimes I could feel him get hard, and I would nervously trace my hand along the outline of his erection.

I wanted to be a girl who boys liked; a girl who boys invited to be their girlfriend. But as seventh grade ended and eighth grade began: I'd still only ever kissed Jared. I'd had dozens of unrequited crushes on dozens of boys (including my silent—though not so secret—crush on Eric Aronson), and I even had a few boyfriends here and there. I wanted Eric to like me back, but he was never my boyfriend. We never kissed, never held hands, and—to this day—never actually spoke about what our bodies did on the playground during recess in seventh grade.

In middle school, girls who kissed a lot of boys were called "sluts," and boys who kissed a lot of girls were called "boys." Daniel Gibson was a boy who kissed a lot of girls. He had a blond bowl cut like Shawn on *Boy Meets World* until one day he buzzed it off and began inviting girls at school to rub his head. Daniel Gibson was a flirt, and it seemed like every girl, myself included, had had a crush on him at least once.

My relationship with Daniel Gibson involved a lot of silence. This isn't to say that we didn't speak—we did. We were friends, I mean to the extent that an adolescent girl can be friends with an adolescent boy who calls her "Torpedo Boobs" and "Shelf Butt" while making *Beavis and Butt-Head*–esque jokes about masturbation. My silence came in the form of never telling him to stop, and his came in the form of never asking me if I thought his jokes were funny (I didn't).

To be honest, I don't actually know if Daniel Gibson ever kissed any girls. Maybe he just talked a good game, his hormones creating the reputation they wished his life would match. But game or not, I believed Daniel was a boy who "hooked up" with girls. I was sure he'd touched lots of boobs, and had lots of girls touch his penis. Fumbling around on the playground over Eric Aronson's jeans, I had come close, but I was now an eighth grader and still hadn't actually touched a penis yet. I decided I should practice, since the real thing might happen any day now.

When I know what I want, and I know the answer will be yes, I am almost never afraid to ask. So I had zero apprehension in asking Daniel Gibson if he would let me give him a practice hand job, and I was not surprised or even excited when he agreed. We both knew going in that this hand job wasn't "real" because I didn't have a crush on Daniel or want him to be my boyfriend or anything like that. I just wanted to practice and needed a willing participant, and Daniel Gibson was a boy who was willing to get felt up by probably any girl who offered.

One night, I invited Daniel and a bunch of our friends to my house to hang out in the basement, which my mom had recently renovated to include a bar, a TV area, and a guest room. Our friends watched a movie and munched on snacks, and Daniel Gibson and I silently retreated to the guest bedroom so I could jack him off. He pulled his penis out of his pants, and I put my hand on it. We didn't speak.

I wanted to be a girl who made boys feel good, so I wanted Daniel to enjoy himself. But I had no idea if he was. He kept closing his eyes or looking off in the distance, like he was trying to concentrate. I worried he was as bored as I was, worried his silence would turn noisy once we left the privacy of that room and he blabbermouthed to everyone about how bad I was at hand jobs. I was not enjoying myself. My mind started to wander as I wondered what I was supposed to be feeling, but I quickly brushed away the thought, reminding myself that *my* feelings weren't what mattered in this moment—right?

I wanted to be a girl who made boys feel good, so I kept

trying. I varied my pace and changed my hand and arm placement until my preteen biceps finally fatigued. Daniel didn't come, and without that rom-com indication that the scene was over—eventually, we both just gave up.

I wanted to be a girl who made boys feel good, so I have no doubt that before we left that room that night, I lied to Daniel Gibson and told him I'd had fun. I'm sure I even thanked him.

Daniel Gibson, Eric Aronson, and I are all friends on Facebook these days. Daniel designs custom bow ties, wears ironic 1980s dad eyeglasses, keeps a handlebar mustache, and probably listens to a lot of vinyl. Eric teaches poli-sci at a state school, is the kind of professor who wears old Ramones T-shirts and scally caps, and posts pictures of dry rubs and meats he's smoking in his backyard pellet grill. As I scroll through their lives on my cell phone screen, I frequently find myself wondering what stories these boys might tell of what they remember about me.

Recently, I made a post about how a boy in middle school used to call me "Seven-head" because of my disproportionately large forehead. *I am SO sorry if that was me*, Daniel Gibson replied.

Maybe his memory is bad, but I doubt it. His comment

proved my suspicion (and quelled my worry) that these boys remember these things just as much as I do. Our hips and butts and bodies on the playground. Our Bazooka bubble gum kisses. The names they called me. I bet Daniel Gibson remembers that preplanned basement hand job too. I want to be a woman who doesn't care what men think of her, but I still wonder if—in his memory—he enjoyed it.

Your forehead is excellent, Daniel's comment continued. *Teenage me didn't know any better . . .*

I know, I replied.

1998

My first real hand job was in a car. It was Logan's car—a sleek, shiny, red, sporty thing that I was probably supposed to be impressed by—and he'd scolded me many times before for touching its exterior. Apparently, touching cars creates microscopic scratches in the paint, and Logan was deeply concerned about the permanent, invisible damage I was creating on his prized possession. I would, many times, jokingly ask why it mattered if the scratches were so small that no one could see them. And Logan would, very seriously, ask me—

again—to please not touch the paint. I wanted to be a girl who made boys laugh, but Logan never seemed to hear any of my jokes.

I was going into the tenth grade, and Logan and his car lived in Grafton, a suburb a few towns over from me. Much of our courting process centralized around him revving his engine as he drove past me and my friends sitting on a public bench, on a strip where boys with cars would cruise by. We would eat Skittles and drink Sprite as they blew marijuana smoke out their windows. They were in high school, too, but these were older boys who knew how to buy beer or vodka to mix with our Minute Maid lemonade and Hi-C Orange at parties. Being Logan's girlfriend involved a lot of me riding around destination-less in his car, which is why understanding that I was not to touch it unnecessarily was imperative.

One night, we went to a bonfire at a friend's house, and Logan asked if I wanted to go to his car. A little drunk, I quipped that it'd be hard for me to get in without touching the paint. If he responded at all, it was by silently taking my hand and walking me toward the street. His invitation was a declaration posed in the form of a question, and the presumed answer was "yes." We sat in the front seats, and I joked about how less optimal of a place this was for making out, as compared to our friend's spacious suburban front yard.

Logan didn't respond to any of my banter. Instead, he leaned across the front seat, brought my hand toward his penis, and asked, *Can you feel that? Can you feel what you're doing to me?*

This was the moment I'd been practicing for that night with Daniel Gibson. I wanted to be here, but I wasn't sure I was "doing" anything other than kissing Logan back, trying to concentrate while staring off into our friend's dark, empty front yard, and getting lost in my head.

Can you feel what you're doing to me?

While the 1990s zeitgeist taught us hardly anything about vocalized consent, we were often reminded that when you don't have anything nice to say, don't say anything at all. But boys never seemed to follow that suggestion. *It ought to be a rule for making out*, I thought to myself, like, if you don't have anything to say about how your partner feels, just don't say anything at all. Can *I* feel what *I'm* doing to *him*? The question hit me like a strange, selfish form of would-be dirty talk. As though the entire purpose of my presence was to create a feeling for his experience. I was still a girl who wanted to make boys feel good, but I was beginning to wonder when it would matter if I was feeling anything at all.

Logan held his hand on top of mine, guiding me to stroke his erection and bending his knuckles over mine to take a full grip.

Put your mouth on it, he whispered. *Just put your mouth on it for a little bit. Just to get it wet.*

As we crossed the threshold from middle to high school, girls who kissed a lot of boys were called "girls," and "sluts" now indicated girls who gave head. Daniel Gibson had taken to saying I had "DSLs" or "dick-sucking lips," but I was nowhere near ready to give a blow job. As far as I knew, only one of my friends had done that before, and I didn't want to get a reputation for being a slut.

I haven't had the chance to practice that! I thought to myself, a smile creeping across my face and a giggle just barely slipping past my lips. I might be bad at it, and the only thing worse than getting a bad reputation for giving blow jobs was getting the reputation for being bad at them.

Logan didn't respond to my giggle, and it was too dark in his car for him to see me smiling. Instead, he put his hand on my hand, harder this time. He let out a warm exhale near my ear, probably believing I would like that. I didn't. But it didn't seem as though any of that—how I was feeling, what I liked, what I didn't like—mattered to him. Logan seemed more concerned with letting me know what *he* liked and how *he* felt.

C'mon . . . Logan groaned, gruffly, softly, breathily. *I don't want to*, I said. But I was still stroking, my arm beginning to tire, my pace slowing. Logan didn't seem to mind. He seemed . . . happy?

Am I happy? I silently asked myself and no one at all. *Is this what happy feels like?*

Uuuuh, Logan breathed. *C'mon* . . . *Spit on your hand. Auuuh, that feels good. Just spit on your hand a little bit, and then do that again.*

Outside of him telling me not to touch the paint on his car, this was probably the longest conversation Logan and I had ever had. I responded with silence. I didn't want to get the reputation of being a slut, I didn't want to get the reputation of being "bad at bed," but I didn't want to be called a prude either. Regardless: spitting on my hand felt like a slippery slope toward a blow job.

I wish I could say that I heard myself that night. Suddenly realized I had a voice, knew I deserved better, spoke up and

asserted to Logan—and myself—what I did and did not want
to do. I wish I could say that I heard myself saying no, even if
that exact word never actually slipped past my lips in the car
with Logan that night. But that's not what happened. Instead,
I calculated a compromise. I asked for Logan's hand, spat there
instead, and watched him finish himself off.

· · ·

If there is one thing that Blake, Jared, Eric Aronson, Daniel
Gibson, Logan, and the dozens of crushes, boyfriends, and
eventual one-night stands I would come to have all had in
common: It's that I decided I liked them before ever knowing anything about them. I'm sure at the time I *thought* I
knew them, but: It's hard to know someone you've never actually communicated with, right? I liked these guys for the
image they projected, how they dressed, how they invited
our bodies to intertwine. I liked them because I wanted to
be a girl who boys liked, and these boys liked me back. And
yet if you asked me to describe what it was about their per-
sonalities that I was *actually* attracted to, I would have little
to tell you.

Instead, what stands out is how I felt as these interactions were happening. The distracted thoughts I had in the moment, the internal acknowledgment of my own silence, and the way I kept trying despite what I was feeling. It's like I believed that with enough practice, I would be ready for the moment when what I was feeling would be at the center of the story I was creating for myself.

These guys aren't memorable for who they were. Instead, I recall them as one among many (perhaps not-so-) microscopic scratches on my psyche. Each one is a milestone on the years-long journey of me allowing my silence to convey me. Betray me. Each one is a lesson I would have to unlearn.

To this day, Logan still lives in Grafton. We are not Face-book friends. The only interaction we've had since I dumped him a few weeks after the hand job was decades later, shortly after the school shootings down in Parkland, Florida, when a mutual friend posted about being afraid for his nephews going to school with armed guards standing watch. I commented that I felt the same way about my sister's kids. Logan jumped on the thread, spouting off about how he would happily join forces with community vigilantes and parroting the conservative ignorance that the only thing that stops a bad guy with a gun is a good guy with a bigger one.

For a moment, it surprised me that he commented without acknowledging how—or even *that*—we knew each other. But maybe Logan no longer remembers me. Maybe his recollection of our relationship has been rubbed out by the feeling every woman who followed me has since created for him. I doubt it, but I honestly wouldn't be upset to learn that this was Logan's truth.

We remember the people and moments that matter, even if we don't always know why or how they matter as they are happening. I want to be a woman who is memorable, but it is entirely possible that Logan has forgotten how I made him feel in his car that night, because what he was feeling didn't really matter: not to me and eventually not even to him.

Oh hi Logan, I wrote back on the thread. *Long time no talk.*

It was a joke since we never really talked, but I don't think he got it. Either way, he said nothing in response.

THIS NIGERIAN'S LIFE

I recently asked some close friends if I'd ever told them how my dad died. *I always assumed he was shot?* one said. *I think it had something to do with his family?* another answered. The truth is: How my father died depends on what—and who— you believe. It depends on how you define the word "truth," and on who might be motivated to tell it. Is there even such a thing as truth? Can there be more than one? How do you define family, blood, community? Does sharing blood make you family? Is community like blood? And what about blame? If there is no blood on anyone's hands, who is to blame for a death?

To understand how my dad died, you also need to understand how he lived—where he's from, how he came to America, how he came to be my dad. The truth, if there is such a thing, exists in both the words and the silence of his story. And I'm old enough now to know that my dad's story changes depending on who's telling it, and who they're telling it to.

When my siblings and I were growing up, our dad told us he was from a small village in Nigeria where, after completing high school, he studied to be a Catholic priest. He told us his bishop decided that the village priest would be even more valuable to the community if he had an American education, so the bishop decided to send my dad to get a bachelor's degree at Marquette University in Milwaukee, Wisconsin. And then, my dad told us, while he was at Marquette, he met my mom in a library (*Checked her out and never returned her*, he would joke). They fell in love, got married, and had kids, so he was therefore unable to become a priest. Instead, my dad told us, he decided to live in America with his wife and growing family.

My dad's retelling of his own life was a simple and carefully crafted true story for when his children asked about where we came from. It was, it seems, the story he told my mom and her family—as she and Uncle Ato tell it to me the same way, to this day. But I now know my dad's story was quite a bit more complicated.

Yes, my dad was born and raised in a small Nigerian village, and yes, he completed studies to become a Catholic priest after high school. But by the time he finished seminary school—sometime around 1965 or 1966—my dad had decided *for himself* that he no longer wanted to be a priest. He wanted to have a family, and he had a girlfriend—Evelyn. Instead of becoming a priest, my dad completed another two years of study to become a teacher (from about 1966 to 1968), and then he worked as a teacher for about a year before immigrating to Milwaukee in 1969.

If we zoom the camera out, the larger story involves the fact that Nigeria won its independence from Britain in 1960, finally severed ties in 1963, held its first elections in 1964, and became embroiled in a civil war in 1967 following a coup in 1966. Like any war, the hows and whys are complicated, disputed, and impossible to detail succinctly. Nigeria's war was cultural. The Igbo (who are sometimes referred to as Ibo, an adapted spelling to make it easier for colonizers to pronounce) wanted to secede and form their own nation. And—in many retellings of Nigeria's civil war—the slaughter of thousands of Christian Nigerians, many of whom were Igbo and neighboring minority tribes like my dad's Ibibio, made it increasingly dangerous to practice Christianity in the region.

If we refocus the lens to what my dad's family and community likely expected of him when he left Nigeria, we would see three things. First, it was expected that he would either return to marry Evelyn or bring her to America to be with him. Second, it was expected that he would send money home to his parents and that his younger and only brother, Thomas, was responsible for receiving and distributing that money. Finally, it was expected that my dad would eventually sponsor Thomas to immigrate to America too. But when the time came for my dad to sponsor his first family member to join him in America, he chose his nephew Eman.

Today, Cousin Eman is in his midfifties. He lives in Minnesota with his wife—also a Nigerian—and their kids. He worked in the manufacturing industry for years, and now owns the company that used to employ him. Eman calls my mom every year on Christmas and Mother's Day. While we don't have much of an independent adult relationship, I love and respect my cousin. As the only living member of my dad's family who has ever spoken to us, Eman can provide insights on my dad's life—and those insights are among my only lifelines and connections to my dad's past.

And so, after asking my mom for Eman's phone number, I

texted to tell him I was writing about my family and childhood and wondering if he had time to chat with me. I knew the story Eman might tell me about who my dad was and how he died would be different from what I'd always been told, if for no other reason than that I'd never been told much of anything. And I was ready to hear it. I had graduated from college. I lived on my own. I had a big girl job, I was writing a book, and I am a whole grown-up now. I could handle it.

Part of me hoped that adult-me talking with Eman would finally be told the truth. But part of me also knew (and has always known) that there isn't any such thing as capital *T* truth. Either way, the text message had already been sent. And Eman responded the very next day.

• • •

Both Eman and my dad were raised to see life and death as being impacted, if not sometimes directed, by the spirit. *Once, Eman tells me after we arrange a time to talk about his memories of my dad, I called Uncle to tell him about a man in my village who had died. When Uncle asked what happened, I told him it was a spirit. The man was at work, got up from his desk, took a few steps, fell over, and died. That was how my father died too*, Eman continued. *One day, all of a sudden, he was just gone. People in the village said that there were wicked ones who were after my father. They were jealous, so they had the spirits kill him.*

Nigerian culture is no more monolithic than American culture is. My dad's tribe, the Ibibio, are neighbors to the Igbo, but they're distinct. As are the Yoruba, and the more than three hundred other Nigerian tribes. The Ibibio tribe is small, insular, and deeply spiritual. They value traditional spirituality first. Respect for one's father, male elders, and male family members comes second. And after years of colonialism and missionaries in West Africa, Christianity likely comes in a close third. Ibibio culture incorporates the belief systems that were forced upon them with the ones that are homegrown. And the existence of spirits, the presence of ancestors, the practice of witchcraft, the use of natural doctors, and the belief in the power of sorcery and juju are standard parts of everyday life.

The Ibibio embraced Christianity the way an American might paint a house. The paint color is a full commitment, something you will see daily, something you might call upon as directions to your home—*the green house at the bottom of the hill.* But house paint is not and never will be more important than the foundation of the building. The foundation is solid, ever present, yet invisible. Wood. Nails. Concrete. Cement and plaster. The foundation is the walls that surround you, the ceiling above you, and the floors beneath. It is part of everything, and it is what keeps everything from falling apart. The Church and its priests were respected, revered, and held up as exemplar members of Ibibio society. But their powers were not greater than that of the spirit and the ancestors.

Yet when Cousin Eman told my dad about the man who'd been killed by the spirit, my dad was incredulous. *Sounds like a heart attack*, my dad said to Eman. *People do not just fall over and die.*

He told me about a man in Wisconsin who died while mowing his lawn one day, Eman recalled of their conversation. *He asked me how I thought that man died, if there are no wicked people who can place spirits on you in America.* "There is no ghost!" *Uncle said.* "People die for medical reasons. They don't die from ghosts."

Cousin Eman, the son of my dad's eldest living sister, has two uncles on his mom's side: my dad and Thomas. Eman has a complete childhood of memories with his uncles. He remembers Evelyn and he remembers staying with my dad during his year of teaching. He remembers how Thomas—also a teacher—once rode his bike for fifteen miles to pick Eman up from school and bring him home for the summer. My dad was always Eman's favorite uncle, and so Eman also remembers my dad leaving for America around the same time Eman's mother began to caution him about war planes flying overhead. I remember my dad talking about Eman. He was a teenager. Really smart. He was going to make something of himself. And we were going to help him.

On the other hand, I cannot remember my dad ever even saying the name Thomas. I have to imagine he wasn't close with his brother, or at least didn't hold him in the same high regard he did their nephew—but maybe that isn't true. I always knew that both of my parents sent money home to their parents, and according to Eman, my dad sent between one and two hundred dollars to his parents, via Thomas—every few weeks. Today, a teacher's salary in Nigeria is just under three hundred and fifty dollars a year: so even in the 1980s and '90s, two hundred dollars a month was a substantial amount of money in Nigeria. Eman recalls my dad once sending him two hundred dollars as well—it was the biggest gift anyone had ever given him. Eman sent my father a note thanking him and wrote about it in a diary that Eman still has to this day.

Uncle wrote back and told me that no one in the family had ever thanked him for sending them anything, Eman tells me. *I wrote about that in my diary too.*

The funds Thomas was responsible for collecting were intended to go to my dad's entire family, and toward the building of a home for the family to live in. By 1989, when my dad's mom visited us in River Falls, my dad had been in America for twenty years and was sending money home to his family whenever he could. But during that visit, it seemed someone, possibly Thomas, had been pocketing the lion's share of the money. Presumably, whoever it was, they thought they'd get away with it.

The money changed him, Eman recalls of his youngest uncle. Thomas had begun to garner a reputation in the village for being a bit braggadocious. He would flaunt his new-found wealth, going to bars and offering to buy the next round of everyone's drinks. *My brother is in America,* Thomas was known to say. *And he is rich!* Presumably, Thomas seemed to think he could spend the money however he pleased, but when my dad found out, he was outraged. *He got on that phone, ohh,* Eman recalls. *You could hear him from a mile away!*

According to Eman, Thomas believed deeply in the power of spirits. It seems that if Thomas were to tell the story of how a man died, it would begin and end with that man's relationship with the ghosts of his past. When an Ibibio parent dies, the custom is for the surviving children to cover the cost of the funeral and burial. Further, the children are expected to host the extended family in the parent's home and to pay them money. The eldest brother or male family member decides how much money is owed and how it will be distributed. Eman was thirteen when his father died, and he remembers: *Everyone came to our home. They ate all the food we had, and they left us with nothing.*

Like the interpretation of any story, a custom being defined as harmful depends on who is asserting that definition. And when I hear something I deem as harmful, it's hard for me to not say anything. My instinct is to push back, to complicate, to ask questions. *But your mom had four kids*, I counter. *Wasn't there concern about what she and her children would eat? And their mourning? Weren't people worried about you all?*

When a man dies, Eman replied, *his wife and children can be put out on the street.* They are no longer part of the family. The man's home and everything he owned now belongs to his family of origin; and his eldest brother or male relative will distribute the belongings as he sees fit to the rest of the family. *They are not worried about the kids,* I hear Eman's wife say in the background of our phone call. *The only worry is what the deceased had and how they can get their hands on it.*

My dad's dad died in 1980—three years before I was born and while my dad was in the middle of his dissertation for his PhD. Contrary to cultural expectations, my dad did not go home for the funeral and didn't have much money to send either. Even as a child, I understood what a great insult this had been to his family. But when, as an adult, I ask Eman if the family was mad about this: He insists they were not. *Everyone understood why Uncle did not come for Grandfather's funeral.* When I remind Eman that I've always been told otherwise, he hedges. *Well, yes. People in the village would not have understood. Yes, they would have questioned it. But in the family—my mom, our grandmother, our aunties Theresa, Affi, and Grace— they all understood.* But in this definition of "all," there is no mention of Thomas.

My dad's mom died just over a decade later, in the middle of the spring semester of 1992. My mom tried to convince my dad—now a college professor—to complete the semester, get his grades out to his students, and meet the rest of his work obligations before going home. While work and school had kept him from his father's funeral, that wasn't an option for my dad when it came to his mother. He began immediately making travel plans.

Several years prior, my dad had a near-fatal accident in a Ford Mustang. He wound up in the ICU in St. Louis, where he was studying for his PhD, and my mom—in Madison for medical school—dropped everything to be by his side. At discharge, my dad had a permanent soft spot on his head from his injuries and a seizure disorder for which he'd be medicated for the rest of his life.

Whenever my mom tells the story of my dad's hospital stay, she recalls how it seemed like maybe he was hallucinating in the ICU—seeing or speaking to something no one else in the room could see. He seemed not like himself and was making cruel jokes to the medical staff even when he was the only one who laughed. My mom recalls apologizing for him, reassuring the nurses that he wasn't normally like this. And one time after his discharge, my dad stopped taking his antiseizure meds, and my mom woke up to him foaming from the mouth in bed next to her. She made him promise never to skip his meds ever again.

In 1992, my dad arrived in Nigeria for his mother's funeral as a healthy, forty-two-year-old man. He still had the soft spot on his head and was still on seizure medications, but he would have completed a recent physical exam to travel. He would have been vaccinated against common illnesses like yellow fever, typhoid, and cholera. He would have been prescribed medications to prevent malaria. My dad's friend Martin, who'd been raised in the same community, warned my dad to take precautions when he arrived. Even a poor American is rich in Nigeria, and political decisions were still made via coups and assassinations. *Not even family*, Martin said, *could be trusted*.

But my dad did trust his family, and had maintained a relationship with them for the last two decades via letters and phone calls. He'd helped his eldest sister by sponsoring her son to come to the States, and—presumably—he had forgiven Thomas for any possible mishaps that might have happened with the money he was sending home all those years. I can almost never hear my dad's voice, and outside of my little sister's wedding, I cannot even remember the last time I've personally set foot inside of a church. But the one snippet of my dad's voice I can still sometimes hear is him reciting the Lord's

Prayer: *Forgive us our trespasses, as we forgive those who trespass against us.*

I remember my dad packing his suitcases with cans of sardines to take for his trip home. Cousin Eman remembers my dad packing his passport, five thousand dollars in cash, our recently purchased camcorder, and his return ticket. *He had Thomas carry all of these things on his person at all times*, Eman recalls, *for safekeeping. And Thomas was very protective of his brother.* When I press Eman for why anyone in the community would need to be protective of anyone else, he reminds me of his own father. Of how people in the community said there were wicked ones after him who were jealous and sought to have the spirits kill him. Maybe, Eman seemed to imply, Thomas was worried that this same fate would befall my father.

During the first week he was away, my dad called us every day. Things were going fine, and plans for the funeral were coming along as anticipated. But then we stopped hearing from him. Something was wrong.

When my mom, her brother, or Eman tell the story of my dad's trip home, their narratives converge on one night, when my dad told his family he was seeing things. No one can say for certain what he saw, because no one else could see them. Was it real? That depends. Do you believe people sometimes see things no one else can see? My mind goes to the soft spot on my dad's head. As a kid, when I touched my daddy's head, my fingers would tenderly come upon that soft spot, and I would check his face to make sure he hadn't winced. I never wanted him to feel pain, not even for a moment, not even if only he could perceive it.

That night in Nigeria, my dad told his family he was afraid. Terrified. They witnessed him blacking out, and when he'd come to he'd say he didn't know where he was. He was losing the ability to track time and place. My mind goes to his nights in the ICU, when—according to my mom and his doctors—he was hallucinating. Was that how his family would have interpreted it? My mind goes to his seizures, to the image of him foaming at the mouth when he and my mom were in bed sleeping. She called 911; what did they do? Finally, my mind goes to Thomas and to the cultural customs when an Ibibio man dies.

For lack of a better word, Eman tells me, *your dad was like Thomas's personal bank.* There was good reason, then, for Thomas to be protective of my dad. With my father alive, Thomas could expect to receive the equivalent of his teachers' salary multiple times over, every year. With my dad alive and both of their parents now dead, Thomas could continue to be a wealthy man.

Now, I myself am not a gambling woman. In my entire adult life, I have purchased a Powerball ticket only once that I can recall. But I am always interested in the decisions of folks who hit it big in the lottery, selecting numbers that—in an instant—make them multimillionaires. Sometimes they'll choose to take that money in small installments over the course of the rest of their lives; and sometimes, now that the opportunity has landed in their laps, they take the lump sum—even if that one-time payout is less than the cumulative installments. Money, and the opportunity to have it, can change a person.

I am filled with fear for my dad when I think of the last days of his life. Filled with rage for how his family responded.

When I go home, Eman tells me, *I tell my sisters I will only eat food I see them make for me.* When I ask why, he says, *Well, people can put things in your food. Someone can be jealous of you and put rat poison or who-knows-what in your food. They can kill you . . .*

As I listen to Eman's voice trail off, I hear his hesitation in admitting that he not only needs to watch his sisters prepare his food; he also requires them to eat from the same dish too.

I have to know we are all eating the same thing at the same time, he says, *because you just never know. You just never know what people can do.*

Eman claims he does not believe in ghosts, and he reminds his sisters of this when he goes home. Presumably, my dad would have agreed with him. But the truth of danger exists whether or not you believe in it, and whether or not anyone else agrees with you. Racism, climate change, a virus—you can say it ain't so as much as you want, but that doesn't make it not true. I can go to Nigeria and tell everyone there is no such thing as malaria, but that doesn't mean I cannot die from it.

My dad was raised to believe that ancestral spirits, ultimately, control everything. For any disrespect to your elders, you will answer to your ancestors. And as much as he grew to believe differently, it's hard to fully shed the skin of your upbringing. So I wonder what—or who—he saw that night in Nigeria. Maybe his father visited him. Or his grandfather. Or the bishop, or the bishop's father. Just because someone helps you, doesn't mean they won't harm you. Just because you trust someone, doesn't mean they are to be trusted. My dad asked Thomas for help; Thomas called in another nephew—David—for assistance.

If Thomas were to tell the story of how a man died, that story would begin and end with that man's relationship to the ghosts of his past. And so, as I've been told: Thomas may have believed that what was happening to my dad was not a medical problem; it was spiritual. Following custom, it seems Thomas and David took my father to the church.

I wonder about this decision. From everything I've come to understand about Ibibio culture: Repentance is due not to God but to your ancestors. But this was the tradition. And in keeping with that tradition, the story goes that Thomas and David took my dad to a series of churches and priests; and to witch doctors and natural medicine people.

The priests, some of whom may have been my dad's friends from seminary school, would have prayed over him. They would have poured holy water on his skin and given it to him to drink. The natural doctors would have mixed herbs and oils into tinctures and teas to feed him. At some point, my dad asked to see a physician, but the doctor turned him away, confirming what it seemed Thomas already believed. *Your problem is not medical*, my dad was told, *it is spiritual.*

This went on for two weeks. Two. Weeks.

I have been told he died at a natural doctor.

WHO I ALWAYS WAS

I have been told he died in a church.

I have been told he died in his family home.

I have been told he died from juju.

I have been told a priest poisoned him with holy water.

I have been told a witch doctor killed him with spirits.

I have been told his family killed him.

I have been told someone in the village killed him.

I have been told a lot of things, but only one thing is true.

Fear can kill you. The brain allows us to believe we're in a different place. We can dream. We can drive ourselves mad. Since the age of nine, I've been told a lot of stories about what happened to my dad. The nuance and the detail has sharpened as I've aged and the storytellers deemed me old enough to know the "truth." But what my mom says and what her brother says and what my cousin says aren't the same, and none of it is consistent. I can audio record the story and tell it to my siblings later, and they will affirm they've been told a different story by the very same person.

No one is lying—it's just that there is no such thing as capital T truth when parsing through the various interpretations of this story. The only thing I've ever been told that has never changed: is that my dad is dead.

A part of me is afraid as I write this, because my dad's ancestors are my ancestors. The spirits who knew him would also know me. As I write I hear a sound outside my door, and it startles me. I sit with my back against the wall, lest anything sneak up over my shoulder. The wind blows, and I watch the leaves on a tree move. I can see my neighbors under their porch lights in the dark of night-night, and I wonder who can see me. I wonder if my ancestors can feel me writing these words. I wonder if my dad's family will ever read these words. I wonder what they think of me.

I have, for most of my life, parroted the narrative that—other than Cousin Eman—my dad's family "stopped speaking to us" after my dad died in 1992. But the truth is, other than Eman and my grandmother: They *never* spoke to us. When my dad was too sick to call home, *no one* called in his stead. No one reached out to tell us what was going on.

It was Thomas who decided no one should tell you, Eman says. *He told me he wanted to protect you, that he did not want you and your mother to be worried. He said he knew what he was doing. And: he said he knew there was nothing you kids, your mother, or her medical doctor training in America could do to help him.*

In the 1980s and '90s, Uncle Ato was a Pan-African community organizer in Milwaukee. It was through his networks that we found out about my dad's death. The news scared my mom's family, and they forbade her from attending the funeral. *They are not a safe people*, she was told. *This juju is nothing to mess around with and not to be taken lightly.*

Instead, Cousin Eman went to Nigeria for my dad's funeral. When he arrived to identify the body, he found his uncle had lost fifty pounds in the three weeks since we'd last seen him. *He looked like he hadn't eaten the whole time he was there*, Eman says. *Or dehydration*, he adds, a defeated *tsk* in his tone. *I kept saying only dehydration could do that to a man*. My mom asked for an American government official in Nigeria to investigate, but the village turned them away. This was a tribal issue, and the tribe would handle it.

From a Black American, fuck-the-police perspective: I can appreciate this. But, like, my dad is dead. As much as I hate being from a country that believes it can somehow solve problems in cultures it does not even understand, I can't help but be pissed off that an investigation didn't happen. Only an external autopsy was conducted, and there were no reports of physical injuries. When Eman observed my dad's body, he could see my dad hadn't been shot, stabbed, or physically wounded. But then again: those methods of an unproven, yet potential murder weren't part of a story anyone was telling.

When he came back to Wisconsin, Eman gave us a video of my dad's funeral, filmed on the camcorder my dad had brought with him on the trip. I don't know how to explain why my mom, my siblings, and I didn't watch it—except to say that she was devastated, and we were children. Uncle Ato is the only person who's ever viewed it, and he says it's hard to watch, hard to see my dad's body be treated in a way he believes is disrespectful. But even when I—as an adult—ask him directly what he means by that, he avoids my question. *Well, maybe they don't see it like that*, he says. *They have their own culture and beliefs, so I cannot tell them what they should or shouldn't do with his body.*

My uncle says something happens in the video—a flash of light or darkness or something he cannot explain. And while I want to have all of my questions answered: I know seeing my dad's funeral isn't going to do that. My memory of my dad lives in my mind and in my heart and in my photo albums. I am protective of those memories. I don't want to risk smudging them by seeing something I won't be able to explain. And just like when my parents would switch into Fante or Pidgin so that child-me and my siblings wouldn't be able to follow what they were saying, I've come to appreciate how not being able to follow the narrative can protect me from a story I might not be capable of understanding.

In the years since my dad's death, Eman's mom has visited him in Minnesota, but as far as I know: She has never asked to meet me, my mom, or my siblings—including my sister who lives less than an hour away from Eman. When I ask why, Eman never really answers my question. Because there is no real answer. My dad's family doesn't speak to us because my dad's death activated a part of their culture not to. End of story.

• • •

In the five years since I first started writing this book, since I first spoke with Eman to better understand my dad's story: all of my dad's sisters (except for Eman's mom) have died. As the eldest male relative in my dad's family of origin, Thomas was always responsible for collecting money from his nieces and nephews and distributing (or keeping) it as he saw fit—and he had already earned a reputation of cruelty when it came to the family's finances.

When one of the sisters was struggling and living in the family home built with my dad's money, Thomas allegedly kicked her out—even though she had nowhere else to stay. And when one of the sisters died and her children did not, in keeping with tradition, have the funds to pay to Thomas: They called Eman for help. By this time, Eman and Thomas hadn't spoken for years, but Eman elected to break his silence to advocate for his cousins. It was all in vain, though, as Eman tells me that Thomas refused to waive tradition and expected them to pay as he had requested.

Years passed, and before any funds were handed over—only months before the final edits of this book—Thomas died.

In the five years since I first started writing this book, since I first sought out to attempt at telling my dad's story: I have come to realize that what I am seeking is a place to neatly direct my blame. A place to fairly direct my anger. But what I have learned, what I have always known, is that this effort is an impossible one.

In the months before the final edits of this book, I asked Eman who, or what, he thinks may have caused my dad's death. *I just don't think he could have done it*, Eman says, knowing where I have—perhaps unfairly—already placed my blame.

Eman compares it to when someone is murdered, and the cops accuse a well-known, local petty thief. *He was a crook*, Eman says of Thomas, *but I don't think he was a killer.*

And yet, just five years ago, when I first set out to be told the truth, I was given what I interpreted as a slightly different story from the very same source. No one is lying, it's just that there is no such thing as capital *T* truth.

•   •   •

Do you think a family member killed him? I asked Cousin Eman bluntly during our initial conversation, five years ago; and I could hear his hesitation again. *I want to believe that is not true*, Eman said, but also tells me that he and Thomas didn't speak for years. When I asked why, Eman responded with a story.

Your mother asked me to bring back the camcorder, he says. *She and Uncle bought it together and were still paying for it on credit. When I asked Thomas for it, he told me no. He said the camcorder, and everything else that belonged to Uncle, now belonged to him. The last two times we spoke, he asked why Auntie hadn't sent him anything for Uncle's death.*

In fact, Eman told me, *Thomas said, "You can tell his wife to sell my brother's home and his car and send the money to me."*

TOYOTAS

After my dad's near-fatal Ford Mustang accident, he resolved to only drive Toyotas. And—because I cling to facets of him like life preservers tossed in a rapidly moving river—I also only drive Toyotas. When I was sixteen, my mom got me a used Tercel, and five years later, when I graduated from college, I inherited my auntie Marie's three-year-old luxury Camry with leather seats, a six-disc CD changer, and a sunroof.

I drove that car until I was thirty-five, and it had well past two hundred thousand miles. When the Camry needed a brake job that would cost more than its Blue Book value, I finally conceded to letting it go. I posted it on Craigslist and sold it for nine hundred dollars to Samuel—a kind-faced, solid-bodied, fortysomething-year-old Nigerian man—who planned to ship it back home for his brother to fix up and re-sell. Samuel said I was beautiful, and he was delighted to learn I am also Nigerian.

Samuel said he'd love to take *me* home to Nigeria too. And—if even for the briefest of moments—I found myself wondering if maybe this was it. Maybe this was my meet-cute. Maybe me and Samuel would fall in love, have a Nigerian wedding, and then buy a house big enough for our family to stay when they came to visit or needed a place to live. Maybe my father had sent me an African just like him, by way of my Toyota.

This was not the first time I'd wondered if I was meet-ing my African Prince Charming. As a teenager and into my early twenties, I convinced myself it was unsafe for me to date African men: on the off chance they might be my extended, unknown relatives. But then I grew up. I stopped conflating all of Africa with a single country. Stopped conflating all of a country with a single community. A single family. A solitary bloodline. But then: The reverse happened. I began to believe I was *destined* to marry another Nigerian. Or Ghanaian. Or West African. Or any African.

In my late twenties, the guy I'd dated while in the Peace Corps in Ecuador was Nigerian. We met on Facebook, and then I proceeded to spend more money than I care to remember on *saldo*, talking to him for endless hours on my Peace Corps–issued cell phone. Winston was in Ecuador teaching English in a city about an eight-hour bus ride from where I lived in Guayaquil. Something about him just felt so intangibly like home—his voice, his silhouette, the roughness of his palms—and the first time we met in person, his cock was in my mouth within thirty minutes. Our relationship lasted nine dramatic, chaotic, loving months: every moment of which I spent vacillating between my deep-seated fear that he would leave me—suddenly and without warning—and my deep-seated hope that I'd finally found the one.

After breaking up with my college boyfriend Blake, I'd promised myself that I was no longer going to be a girl who wasted her time sobbing her eyes out on the phone with her boyfriend. And yet here I was almost five years later: sobbing on the phone with Winston over things so petty I cannot even recollect the details anymore today. *Why* I was crying or afraid or anxious doesn't matter—what matters is *that* I felt that way. Except at the time, the only thing that mattered to me was to be received by somebody who I'd convinced myself I was destined to be with. I didn't know it then, but: love shouldn't require you to give so much.

• • •

My third and final attempt at donating blood happened when I was twenty-seven. I'd just moved to Boston and was working in an office building near Fenway Park when I saw signs announcing the office's annual blood drive. I signed up immediately.

I had—twice—attempted to donate blood while I was in high school. Each of those times, the volunteer nurses told me that my body is not capable of giving. My blood leaves my veins so slowly that, in the maximum amount of time the American Red Cross will allow for you to fill the donor blood bag, I don't even get to the halfway point. It—the attempt to give and my failure—makes me feel like shit. I get woozy and nauseous, like I'm going to pass out. But I want it. I *want* to be a blood donor, and the fact that some authority—the Red Cross or my body—had told me "No" just did not register.

And so, at twenty-seven years old, I signed up for the blood drive at my office. When the day came, I took the elevator up to the designated floor, accepted my clipboard, and began to fill out the predonation survey—hoping that maybe my body had changed. I thought little of the question asking if I'd ever had sex with someone from Africa—the form as specific as my adolescent mind or my early-twenties heart. I simply checked "Yes" and moved on to the next question. Then, during the in-person interview to review the survey, I was asked to elaborate. *Which countries?* the volunteer nurse asked me.

I paused. I looked up at the fluorescent lights on the ceiling and weighed the option of telling this stranger the full truth about how many nations of men I'd allowed between my legs.

Nigeria, Uganda, and Ivory Coast, I answered honestly.

Almost immediately, I was told I would not be allowed to donate blood. The nurse said there was a stream of HIV in Nigeria so aggressive and so resistant to treatment that it was just not worth the risk to the American blood supply. It did not matter that Winston and I had always used a condom. It did not matter that I'd never tested positive for HIV, including in the two years since I'd last seen Winston. They didn't even ask. What was in Nigeria, and what was therefore maybe inside of me, was a danger that did not require further detail.

My dad is from Nigeria, I told the volunteer nurse, my disappointment manifesting itself as a lump in my throat and a prickle behind my eyes. *Same with my ex-boyfriend.*

Oh... I'm so sorry... the nurse stammered, and I recognized their tone. The same one folks take when they apologize for my dad being dead, it's the I'm-sorry-your-life-is-like-this tone.

It's okay, I replied, almost instinctively. *None of this is your fault.* It wasn't anyone's fault.

The volunteer nurse smiled faintly before swiveling in their chair to turn around and fish out a T-shirt to give me from a box under their desk. "Kiss me, I'm a blood donor," the T-shirt lied. And I was sent back down the elevator to return to my desk.

⋅ • • •

A decade after Winston, when I was selling my Toyota to Samuel, I'd like to say I was wiser. I'd like to say I knew better than to throw myself at any man—African or otherwise—who told me I was beautiful and said he wanted to take me home. But, of course, I wasn't—or at least not entirely. I was less consumed with being the kind of girl who boys would like, and I no longer believed that giving myself away would result in someone wanting to receive me, make a home with and for me. But I still got off on the feeling of being wanted. Of being desired.

Once Samuel's check cleared, I invited him back over for a drink. I had roommates, so we opted to watch TV in my bedroom.

Samuel asked what tribe I was from. *Ibibio*, I told him. *I think it's sorta like a subset of Igbo, but I'm not really sure. I don't know a lot about my dad's side of the family.* Samuel asked why not.

My dad died when I was young, I said, knowing what would come next.

Oh, I'm so sorry, Samuel said, right on cue.

It's okay, I replied, internally smiling at my instinct. *You didn't kill him.*

Samuel didn't seem to know how to respond, so he didn't. Instead, he said: *Igbos are not to be trusted. If I were sitting in a room with an Igbo*, he continued, placing his wallet on my ottoman, *I would never leave my wallet out like this. They would take it*, he said as he made a snatching motion with one hand. *That's how they are. As soon as I turned my back they would take it.*

Beyond sharing similar letters, the Igbo and Ibibio are not related. But Samuel seemed content to go along with my error, and—at the time—I didn't know enough about Nigeria to correct his slightly veiled accusation. I didn't know how to defend my bloodline, so instead a little switch went off inside me. *Oh, you think we're thieves?* I thought to myself. *I'll show you a thief.* Justified, I felt content to take what I wanted.

I watched Samuel nurse his cocktail and wondered how long it would be before we could fuck. As he sat in my Ikea rocking chair, I imagined myself straddling him. I imagined his body pounding into my open legs, his tongue on my breasts. I imagined his cock in my mouth as though Samuel's semen swimming in the back of my throat would give me what I'd always been seeking. As though his skin under my fingernails would get me closer to my own blood.

I waited for Samuel to finish his drink. Then I fucked him on my bed covered with a Nigerian purple-and-orange floral print bedspread that I'd made for myself. After he left, I lay in my bed, satisfied and staring up at the ceiling. I was both empty and full. When Samuel texted and called and asked to see me again, I told him I wasn't interested. I'd taken what I wanted, although admittedly: I'd wound up with nothing.

• • •

Once—in some sliver of time sandwiched between the Red Cross at my Fenway office and Samuel in my bedroom—a phlebotomist conducting a routine blood draw told me that

I have tough skin. *What do you mean?* I responded, trying to look him in the eye, trying to break the attentiveness with which I was watching the blood slowly moving from my arm into a little test tube that some machine would spin around or centrifuge or do whatever it is that blood tests do with my insides.

Your skin is thick, he said. *Physically thick. It was hard to get my needle inside you.*

Oh . . . , I choked out in response, turning the idea over in my mind. It felt like suddenly, more than just the soft flesh of my inner arm was exposed to this man. Like he knew. Like he could tell. Like he could see my guards fly up, watch my slow release, interpret my yearn to connect from the eagerness with which I watched my insides escape me.

I wonder now if the volunteer nurse at my office blood drive could see it too. I wonder if Winston could feel it every time his body entered mine. Do my pores sweat it out? Could Samuel or anyone else who visits my body or bedsheets smell it—lingering there?

That longing, eagerness; my desire to give, to be received. I wonder if it's written all over my face, all over every clipboard of paperwork I complete; wonder if it's written in my blood.

PART THREE

(UN)RESOLVED

I moved out East when I was twenty-seven, blindly applying to jobs in Boston because I felt like my soul was telling me to live there. I signed a lease on the first in-budget place I could find: a makeshift attic apartment in the suburb of Newton. I lived there for two years before moving to Boston's neighborhood of Roslindale once I had a better lay of the land. Newton was cute and all, but it was too White and felt too much like suburban Wisconsin. Roslindale was racially and economically diverse, friendly, and (at the time, at least) affordable—in part because of a decades-old shooting (where, side note: a Black man was wrongfully accused and then spent years of his life incarcerated because the American injustice system is fraudulent. There is a whole Netflix documentary about this particular case, and I fully recommend you watch it!).

My first place in Roslindale was, essentially, in a therapy office. I lived in the second story of a two-family home, and my landlord lived downstairs. The second-floor bedrooms were used for her therapy practice: a waiting room, the therapy room, and a file room. The rest of the second-floor unit was, for the most part, mine.

It was written into my lease that between the hours of 7 a.m. and 11 p.m., I would enter from the back porch only. The door at the top of the back steps opened into my apartment's eat-in kitchen with a walk-in pantry. There was a bathroom in a side hallway, then the dining room, and finally a living room through a pair of French doors.

I placed a vintage table with chrome legs in the kitchen, surrounded by three kitchen chairs I'd found on the street and DIY reupholstered with colorful fat quarters from Jo-Ann and nails hammered to a 90-degree angle because I didn't own a staple gun. I transformed the pantry into a craft room, and set up a reading nook in one of the dining room corners, carefully placing an oversized chair from Savers and a little bookcase I'd dragged in from the street and painted bright yellow.

The living room boasted giant bay windows overlooking the front yard, and overlooking the side yard was a sunporch— which I'd made my bedroom. I didn't have a bed frame, so my mattress just sat on top of a split box spring on the floor.

I'd spent weeks looking for the perfect living room couch on Craigslist before finally finding it: a salmon-colored suede camelback that I bought from an elderly couple who was downsizing. I hired a Craigslist delivery guy to transport the couch to my new place. But when he arrived it wouldn't budge through the door—so we sawed off a leg and put it back together again with metal fasteners he luckily had in his truck. *You're not the first lady to fall in love with a couch that doesn't fit,* he told me. *I come prepared now.*

The house was almost a hundred years old. It had crystal doorknobs and creaky floors and sat on a block with several single- and two-family homes, a mix of renters and home-owners. Most nights, I would snuggle into the couch with an Ecuadorian alpaca blanket wrapped around me as I watched *The Colbert Report.* Then I'd retreat to my sunporch bedroom and fall asleep to the sound of neighborhood kids playing in the street, or bachata music when a Latinx family moved in next door.

But my landlord would regularly complain when I "walked too heavily" or would call me at work when I'd forgotten to clean my lint from the dryer in the basement. On the other hand: she baked fresh bread and shared it with me and she filled my early evenings with beautiful tones from her cello practice. So much about my first Roslindale apartment made no sense at all, but I loved living there so I was determined to make it fit my life—determined to make it make sense. Besides: The rent was hella cheap. And did I mention the French doors and crystal doorknobs?! The place was gorgeous.

. . .

A few months after moving to Roslindale, I met Caleb on Ok-Cupid. He lived in Rossie (or Rozzi, or Rozzy—it's a whole thing, let's not get into it), too, except his place was in a new-build, gated subdivision with a big swan on the entryway sign. I hadn't even seen a subdivision since I graduated high school, and it was a bit odd to find this vestige of my suburban youth in my self-selected, adult, city home. At Caleb's place, I had to show my driver's license to a guy at the gate when I went over to visit. Caleb had a roommate who was nice enough but whose presence afforded little privacy. And he didn't have a carefully curated suede salmon-colored couch or a reading nook or salvaged furniture turned beautiful.

D'ya ever notice, I playfully asked him once, *how anyone could live here? I mean, you walk into my house, and it tells you: Theresa lives here. But there's sorta nothing about your apartment that says: This is Caleb's place. Nothing except you being in it, I guess.*

It wasn't an entirely fair critique since it was a shared space, which meant Caleb and his roommate needed to cocreate to fit both of their aesthetics. But it didn't seem like these dudes were even trying. *The rent's not bad,* Caleb said, and shrugged.

I was attracted to Caleb the moment I saw his profile. He stands a few inches taller than me, is seven years older than me, and shaved his head bald because he got tired of fighting his hair loss. I love that in a guy, that this-is-who-I-am kind of confidence. Plus, he had a perfectly groomed light-brown beard peppered with blond strands that felt fantastic in my fingertips. Caleb wore glasses, straight-cut jeans, cute sneakers, and a button-up or a T-shirt under a zip-up hoodie almost every day. It was wintertime when we first started dating, and on a snow day after our second date, Caleb made stew in his Crock-Pot and then walked several blocks in the snow to share it with me.

When we spoke, Caleb looked me straight in the eye so that I knew he was listening. I was just about to turn thirty; I was jaded and guarded, but I trusted Caleb in a way that felt almost instinctual. Falling for him came easily.

I figured I was growing up, gaining a more mature sense of self and of what I needed and wanted in a partner. I'd had plenty of practice doing things the wrong way. I'd spent years going on countless first dates with guys who fell hard for me, while I felt nothing in return. I had pined after guys who probably forgot about me the minute they got to their T stop on the way back home to the rest of their life. I'd abandoned my home for a night in the fuckpad of a guy who had a girlfriend and lied to me about it; I'd shared a month of my life with a guy who would tell me he was falling in love with me as he fucked me on my mattress and split box spring on the floor of my Newton attic, and then went home to the wife he'd assured me he'd divorced, and the child he'd never mentioned.

Maybe I've paid my dues, I told myself. Maybe I'd gone through all of those experiences so that when a guy as good as Caleb came trudging through the snow and into my home, I'd be ready to find a way to make our lives fit together.

I hadn't dated anyone I was serious about since almost five

years prior, when I was still in the Peace Corps, and Caleb felt different than Winston had. I started introducing Caleb to my friends. Our fights were rare and productive. Caleb didn't provoke my usual, constant, and vague fear that my open heart would be left behind, suddenly and without warning. It was like a switch inside of me had flipped. Like he was showing me what was possible when I let the right person into my life, so I let him in.

Caleb was the first guy I invited to see me tell a story onstage. The first person I told when I quietly decided I wanted to become a yoga teacher. I introduced Caleb to my mom, and he introduced me to his dad—and every year, I'm reminded of the occasion when my Facebook Memories show a status update reading "thank god for the little black dress." With Caleb, I always felt like the ground beneath me was steady and predictable. I felt safe.

Caleb was a music teacher at a Boston public school serving mostly students of color who lived in Dorchester and Mattapan, and I was proud to have a boyfriend who taught an artistic elective at a public school serving Black and brown kids. Sometimes Caleb would lament about how it felt like his students didn't really care about music class, or how it seemed like the other teachers didn't respect his position. But I knew how

much classrooms like his meant to me when I was in school—
even though I wasn't the kind of kid who went around telling
my teachers that they mattered to me. Still, I spent many of
my high school lunch hours in the art room working on various projects and assignments. I dropped AP Physics my senior
year, and took an independent study in jewelry instead. My art
teacher encouraged me to apply for art school, and when I first
moved to Roslindale, I was still wearing pieces of jewelry I'd
made in her classroom. I know how important it was to have
had a teacher who believed in me as a creative being, and I was
sure that Caleb was that teacher for his students. It was one of
my favorite things about him.

I invited Caleb to my thirtieth birthday party at a local
karaoke bar. We'd been dating for about four months. He
cheered me on when I sang a drunk-and-off-tune rendition
of Melissa Etheridge's "I'm the Only One," and he fit in easily with my whole extended crew. I would wander off around
the bar checking in on different pockets of friends, and Caleb
would catch my eye from across the room, hold it as he smiled
at me and pursed his lips to blow a corny kiss or wink at me.
He would sling his arm around my neck, kiss me, and hold my
hand while he ordered my drink. Walking home that night,

Caleb said he just wanted to remind everyone in the bar that he was with me, the cutest girl in the place.

That summer, Boston Public Schools refused to guarantee Caleb a job for the next year. He was a first-year teacher and the union allowed for those with more seniority to bump him if they wanted to make a move. Preemptively, Caleb interviewed at a school in the suburbs. They had a big budget for electives and a band he could become the conductor of, and he could chaperone the students on annual trips to New York City.

Sure, I said, *that sounds nice and all. But . . . aren't those kids, like . . . mostly all White? And, like, rich? Or at least almost rich? I mean, why would you want to teach there when these kids from Dorchester and Mattapan really need you, you know? I'm sure BPS will come around.*

I knew he heard me, but my opinions about where Caleb worked the next school year didn't seem to matter to him. It's not like I was ready for us to get married, but I had started to imagine what it would be like for us to build a life together. We would buy a small, cape-style house on Poplar Street in Roslindale. We would get a dog. We would cook stews together in the Crock-Pot in the kitchen, and lounge together on carefully curated vintage furniture under alpaca blankets in a room intentionally accented with his nerdy knickknacks. Maybe we would cocreate some sort of yoga-and-music program to serve Black and brown kids in our community.

As safe as Caleb made me feel, I still held back on sharing any of these "plans" with him. Things were going so well, and part of me was worried that I might break it. Worried that what we had was more fragile than what I was telling myself. Still, I was feeling somewhat certain that Caleb was imagining plans that were similar to mine. I was contemplating a career change to yoga, sleeping on a mattress without a bed frame, and still figuring myself out—but I was happy. Caleb's consideration of a job in the suburbs struck me as nothing more than him just figuring himself out too. I figured this was something we had in common. Something we would keep doing—together.

But, within a few weeks, it was becoming clear that Caleb had a different plan in mind. And he was suddenly completely certain about what he wanted. And what he didn't want.

BPS eventually came around and offered Caleb his job back, but he'd already accepted the new job. He signed a lease on a one-bedroom-plus-study in the suburbs and moved out of Roslindale.

Caleb's suburban apartment clearly announced, *Caleb lives here*, to anyone who entered. He'd fully furnished and intentionally decorated, even transforming the study into a music room full of his nerdy knickknacks. The weekend after I visited Caleb's new place for the first time, he drove to my place in Rossie and waited for me to open the door for him at the back porch. I thought we would be hanging out for the day, but when I got to the bottom of the stairs, his face told me he had other plans. *What's wrong, baby?* I asked. He frowned.

Caleb said he couldn't see himself marrying me. He said even though we were happy now, he knew he wouldn't be happy with me long-term. His voice wavered, and I could see him swallowing hard in his throat, but his eyes were clear and dry. I asked him if he was sure, but I wasn't going to ask him why or demand he explain his feelings. I respected him more than that, and besides: Who was I to assume that how I felt was right and how he felt was wrong?

My life has trained my face to stay still in times of crisis. In fact, I once had a guy break up with me, and then ask if I was sad because he couldn't tell from my face. I slip into a stoic face and stilled feelings without even noticing when I'm doing it.

I learned it from my mom. I've practiced it as a social worker and as a yoga teacher, and I was practicing it in that moment with Caleb. I know better than to let my emotions spill all over every guy who tells me he's just not that into me. Instead, I listened to Caleb say how he felt and I looked him in the eye so he knew I had heard him. I swallowed the tears building up in my eyes and choked down any words of protest my mouth might have wanted to utter.

I hate to sound like every contestant to ever appear on *The Bachelor*, but getting dumped by Caleb blindsided me. It hit me like a sucker punch to my gut. I'd let my guard down with this guy, opened myself up despite my fears. I never told Caleb I was in love with him, and in retrospect: I can't say I ever fully was because I'm not sure it's possible to be in love with someone who doesn't love you back. But my feelings for Caleb were as real as they had ever been for anyone, and it felt like love at the time. Caleb broke my heart that day, and like he'd said himself: We were happy. I just did not see this coming.

Caleb and I hugged, and then I closed the door and went back upstairs to my apartment. I walked through the kitchen, grabbed the box of tissues from the bathroom, landed on the salmon-colored couch, wrapped myself in an alpaca blanket, and didn't move for the rest of the day. I texted my friends, salved my wounds with their shock, and texted Caleb to ask if he could please drop off my library books I'd left at his apartment. A few days later, I came home, and the books were neatly arranged in a brown paper sack on the back porch. There was no note in the bag.

• • •

The first girl Caleb dated after me was a social worker from Wisconsin, just like me. I know this because I would regularly look him up on Facebook (even after we'd unfriended each other), and I was vexed. *How DARE he date another social worker? And she's from Wisconsin?! Fuck him and fuck her, too, bitch, what am I . . . replaceable?!* I decided to take a break from Facebook-stalking Caleb for a while.

When I resumed, about a year later, Caleb's social media revealed he was single again. He would post pictures of the music room in his new apartment, and images of his new classroom. Shiny brass instruments and sharp-looking band uniforms. A big empty space with rows of music stands, his single stand at the bottom, front and center. I scrolled through Caleb's cache of images from those annual trips to New York. My high school band had gone on a trip to the East Coast too. It was the first and only time I visited Boston before moving here. We ate lunch in the cafeteria at Harvard (which isn't even in Boston!) and then headed to New York to see off-Broadway shows, and then to DC, where we were in a parade.

I bet Caleb's kids love that trip as much as I loved mine, I would say silently as I observed his experiences from my cell phone. It became soothing to see Caleb living his life, like watching a stranger at a coffee shop, sipping from their cup and smiling to themselves as they turn the page of a book.

I liked observing Caleb living out his narrative, but after a while, I would have to remind myself to check in on him. He doesn't post much, and I was moving on, dating new people. Bigger and bigger chunks of time would pass without me thinking of him until one day—six, almost seven years after we broke up—I checked Caleb's Instagram and saw he was engaged. He looked so happy! His fiancée has a kind face; she looks bookish and smart. I wondered how they'd met. Maybe she was a teacher at the same school. She looked like an English teacher or maybe the school's librarian: a polite brunette with cute glasses and neutral outfits. I loved the way they smiled at each other. They went to video game conventions and cosplayed as their favorite characters. They wrapped Christmas presents and put them under the tree. For their honeymoon, they went to Universal Studios, took pictures all over the Harry Potter area, and wore coordinating Hogwarts house T-shirts: Hufflepuff and Ravenclaw.

Sometimes when I look at Caleb and his wife—or at any of my exes and their new partners—I feel a tinge of sadness. I want that. Not the guy, I don't want any of those guys anymore. But I want a person who looks at me like that in photos. I want a person who cares about the stuff I care about. I want a person. A partner.

But I cannot imagine being Caleb's wife. I do not want to live in the suburbs, and I do not want to go to game cons. I do not know what my Hogwarts house is, and I do not care. There is nothing *wrong* with that life, but Caleb was right to know that it was the life he wanted to live, and not the kind of life I would ever want to cocreate. When Caleb got married, I was the same age he'd been when we broke up, and there was something about that realization that just made sense. Maybe that's why Caleb knew we wouldn't work out so much sooner than I had. Maybe I was finally old enough to get it. Merely being happy and wanting to be somewhere doesn't mean you can make yourself fit that place. And really: you shouldn't have to force it at all.

That year, I started dating a fellow storyteller named Christopher, whom I'd first become aware of by way of Facebook's "People You May Know" feature. I'd moved out of the therapy office and into my second Roslindale apartment: a place where I could spread out, use any door I wanted at any time of the day without ever having to tiptoe around the creaky wood floors lest my landlord wake up and complain. My bedroom was the size of my entire first apartment in Newton, and I shared a similar aesthetic (or just had a more dominant personality) to my roommates, so I'd taken the liberty of decorating most of the common spaces.

Christopher was quite a bit taller than I was, sort of heavy-set in a stocky way. He was bald and had a beard. I loved his sharp but casual style, and the sly way he smiled at me. Christopher had a not-embarrassed-about-being-a-Black-nerd vibe going on, and I love that in a guy. That this-is-who-I-am kind of confidence. I'd been meaning to go to one of his shows so I could hit on him and ask him out. When I finally got around to it, I'd been home sick all weekend with a cold.

My head cold had robbed my sense of taste, but I was tired

of being in bed and hungry for human connection. I went to the story slam, ordered the house wine because I couldn't taste it anyway, and flirted and bantered with Christopher after the show. The next day I sent him a PM on Facebook, and when he responded, I asked if he'd like to see a show *together* sometime. There was no part of me that doubted he would say yes. My cold in no way hampered my confidence. I was cute; he was cute; and we were both into storytelling. Plus, it seemed like we had a similar sense of humor. That was enough of a foundation for a first date for me.

We went to a comedy show on our date, and then to a restaurant in Rossie for a drink. It was snowing, and the place was empty but for us. We sat at the bar with our knees touching and I drank a Hendrick's gin and tonic with extra limes. Christopher ordered a Bulleit rye on the rocks (and I was relieved because one time a guy on Tinder told me his go-to drink was a "Bailey's no ice," and I had to tell him we could never speak again because who the fuck just drinks half a cup of cream at room temperature?!).

Christopher and I giggled about nothing while the bartender pretended to not overhear our awkward first date chatter. I told him about how I taught yoga in homeless shelters, how I loved vintage shopping, and how I was nurturing a budding passion for cocktails, glassware, and ice. Christopher listened and asked questions. He told me about his job at a bank that he didn't love but that paid well, how he got into storytelling, and how he was teaching himself to play the harmonica. I listened and asked questions. Once, when we were texting between dates, Christopher said I reminded him of Ms. Frizzle from the Magic School Bus books. *Ms. Frizzle with a fro*, he said. *And I mean that as a compliment.* As if it could have been interpreted in any other way!

On our third date, Christopher invited me back to his place, and he played me harmonica versions of pop songs—Maroon 5 and Bruno Mars. I like harmonica just fine, but it felt a bit cringe to be serenaded by a twangy version of Adam Levine's words. *Calm down!* I told myself. *Give the guy a chance and get to know him. He's being nice*, I tried to remember. *This is nice.*

We spent much of that date playing a silly "Ask Me a Question" game, and Christopher was surprised by how quickly I knew which animal I would be: *a hippo—because: curvy, lazy, ferocious*, or what superpower I would have: *invisibility with teleporting—because: duh.*

The next weekend, I invited Christopher over for a drink

and to watch *Saturday Night Live*. I had an early flight home on Sunday morning to meet my newest nephew—my little sister had just had her first baby—and I wanted to spend some time with Christopher before heading out for a few days. I liked to think of myself as a Pandora-of-drinks, and I prided myself on paying attention to what kind of cocktails my friends ordered at bars so I could later anticipate and fulfill their request before they even uttered it. But after two years of keeping a full bar at home, I still never had rye whiskey on hand (because rye is gross—there, I said it, sorry not sorry!), so I couldn't have Christopher's go-to drink ready for him when he arrived. I prepped him a shaken bourbon, straight up, instead.

It was 2019. The Michael Jackson documentary had recently come out on HBO, and the *Surviving R. Kelly* docuseries was airing on Lifetime. That week, R. Kelly had acted a dangerous fool in his interview with Gayle King, and *SNL* was all over it.

It wasn't hard for me to mute R. Kelly, I told Christopher during a commercial break, *since I never really listened to him anyhow. But*, I continued after a sip of my brandy old-fashioned, *I just don't know what to do about Michael Jackson.*

What do you mean? Christopher asked, and added: *You don't have to do anything.*

I gave him a side-eye. *Of course I do,* I said, raising an eyebrow. *We all do. We all have to decide if we're going to keep listening to him or not. I mean, can you imagine what it would be like to be one of his victims, and have your abuser be so openly beloved? And he helped all of their careers! Like, they must feel they owe that to him, but still. He hurt those kids, man, he hurt those kids. It's just such a mess. This whole fucking world is just such a fucking mess.*

We don't know that he hurt anyone, Christopher said as *SNL* came back from commercial.

Pffft, I snorted. *You can't actually believe that.*

After the last skit, Christopher was still nursing his bourbon, and I was wondering if we were going to make out or if I was going to have to find a way to eloquently ask him to leave so I could go to bed.

I'd had a drink. This was our fourth date. We hadn't done more than kissing, and it didn't seem like Christopher was gonna make the first move. *I'm not gonna be tired on this flight for no reason,* I thought to myself.

I pulled the trigger.

So . . ., I said, sipping on nothing but melted ice. *What is this? Like . . . what are we doing here? How are you feeling about me?*

::shots fired!::

The look on Christopher's face revealed that he was as equally trained at neutralizing his reactions as I was. He sighed. Popped another M&M from my bowl of snacks into his mouth. Took a sip of his bourbon. *Well*, Christopher started, *it seems to me that social justice is, like, the most important thing to you. It's almost as though justice is the lens through which you see everything you look at.*

Wow! I thought, a smile blind to red flags slipping across my face. *It's only been four dates and this guy really* gets *me!! Must have been the hippos . . . ?*

And, Christopher continued, *I'm just not sure how I feel about that.*

Gulp. Choke. Cough. Excuse me. Whaaaat?

You're not sure how you feel about what? I said. *About justice? Or are we still talking about how you feel about me . . . ?*

I just feel like I'm not woke enough for you, Christopher said.

I wanted to say: Anyone who would say that shit out loud, for sure isn't. I took a sip of my brandy instead. *Oh?* I replied. *What do you mean?*

I knew, of course, that this had nothing to do with hippos. Christopher liked me. He liked my style. He thought I was talented. He liked my vibe. But I was beginning to see a mirror to my past in Christopher's present. It was like he was trying to make it work with us because he liked the *idea* of us, the idea of me. Or at least—he thought he did.

I just feel like you pressure me to take a side, Christopher said. *Like with Michael Jackson or R. Kelly. I just don't think I should have to make a choice about everything. I don't think I should always have to* do *something.*

Well, I said, *that is literally the choice you are making. Doing nothing is doing something. Also, why are we still talking about Michael Jackson . . . ?*

I like you a lot, Theresa, Christopher responded. *I just can't have these kinda conversations all the time. The cops. The president. The news. Whatever. I just can't talk about it* all *the time.*

I'd already forgotten that on his way over, Christopher had been stopped by the police. He was a bit rattled when he arrived, still worried about what could have happened during that encounter. Standing in my foyer, he'd shaken his head as he told me about it, like he was trying to flick it from his memory. I'd exhaled a sigh as he leaned in to kiss me hello. *Fuck the police,*

I'd whispered into his lips—a budding abolitionist's sweet-sweet nothings. As I pulled away, smiled, and looked Christopher in the eye, I could see something. But I wasn't sure yet what it was. Now, hours later in my bedroom as Christopher told me that he couldn't have "these" conversations all the time, it finally clicked.

One of my favorite things about hippos is that they can't actually swim. A baby hippo can weigh more than a hundred pounds, but their legs are only a few inches long. Imagine keeping yourself afloat with a body like that. Hippos aren't built to swim; they just love the water. So they dive in, exhale, and relax until they hit the bottom, and then they push themselves against it to propel their bodies forward and upward. Hippos are animals who seek out a place where they don't quite fit, and then adapt because it's where they want to be. In the breakup with Caleb and the years since, I'd realized that shared values were absolutely fundamental to me feeling connected to another person—romantically or otherwise. I could buy rye and keep it in the bar for Christopher when he came over because I can adapt and compromise to the place where I want to be. But I'd have to *want* to be there, first. And I didn't want to be in the place Christopher seemed to be offering me. So: maybe this had everything to do with the hippos.

Oh, Christopher, I said, trying not to let a giggle slip. *That means you don't like me. It's okay, though. This is just who I am. It's okay if you don't like it.* He hesitated before responding: *Maybe I should go?*

Yeah. I think you should.

The next morning, I arrived home to Milwaukee and met my brand-new nephew. He was sleepy and cozy and snorty and perfect, and I loved him immediately. When I told my mom and little sister about my last date with Christopher, my mom replied: *That's weird. Why would he say that? Was he raised by the Whites?* He was, but I don't think that's necessarily what mattered here. Christopher and I were just two very different people. We weren't a good fit.

I imagine my ideal partner as someone who will co-hold my narrative with me. Like, have you ever had a thought and then had absolutely no one to share that thought with? I want someone to share thoughts with. Which is to say that I want someone who wants to hear my thoughts, who wants to tell me their thoughts, and who has thoughts I would also want to hear.

I often describe my love language as rides to and from the airport. Christopher did not offer to take me to Logan for my trip home to Milwaukee, and I didn't mind and certainly did not ask him to, because as far as I was concerned: Our relationship ended when he left my house that night. He texted when he knew I'd be taking off and landing, and he checked in and asked about the baby a few times, but I just let it fizzle out and sort of stopped responding. I knew he was just trying to be nice, but nice wasn't enough.

• • •

I no longer sleep on a mattress over a split box spring on the floor. I take Ubers to and from the airport, and it's not unusual for me to have no one to text coming in and out of airplane mode. I try not to hum along when an MJ song plays at the grocery store, and I haven't listened to R. Kelly since 2019 (although I will admit that the challenge of living without "Remix to Ignition" is one I'm not sure I'll ever overcome). My home is filled with kitschy, vintage knickknacks, and you will still never find a bottle of rye in my bar.

But these days, I know better than to claim I know exactly what I want. I still daydream about owning a cape-style house on Poplar Street in Roslindale, but with the nine months of dating Caleb continuing to rank among the longest and most successful of my adult relationships, I know that I need more than mere consensus on what neighborhood we want to live in.

I can't predict and don't bother to articulate what my life will look like in the future, or even what it might look like next year.

But I know what it's *not* going to look like.

NOT ALL PLANTS
GET TO GROW UP

Years ago, a neighbor gifted me a few strands of pothos and a single strand of arrowhead vine in an emptied-out and then water-filled "Two-Buck Chuck" Trader Joe's wine bottle. They'd been cut from their mother plant—a robust and overgrown tangle in a terra-cotta ceramic pot—which she also gifted me. I transferred the Two-Buck Chuck strands to a (much prettier and more sculptural) St-Germain bottle and made them the centerpiece of my dining room table.

Over the course of several weeks, the leaves in the St-Germain bottle became less and less vibrant. When I made dinner or crafted a cocktail in my home bar, I'd hesitate to take #FoodPorn photos for the 'gram with the vines in the background, lest anyone in the comments section tell me I was doing something wrong. And once, during my birthday party, a friend remarked on how the plant needed dirt—or at the very least a larger volume of water—to flourish. This was not news to me.

In its position on my dining room table, the St-Germain centerpiece reminded me of the still-life unit from my high school art classes. We would walk into the art room and find Mrs. Grant had placed a bowl of fruit at the center of each four-person table. Smudging charcoal or colored chalk, we each created our own versions of the centerpiece from our individual vantage points. Week after week the bowls would return, and since the fruit was fake, it never rotted. I'm not sure I've ever seen a still life of a rotting or dead centerpiece. Despite being suspended in time, a still life always looks alive. But real life isn't still. Real life involves—*requires*—growth.

Every day, I would walk past the vines in the St-Germain bottle and sigh. The leaves, alive and still turning to face the dining room window, had begun to pale like a photograph slowly fading in the sun's light. But the roots were strong, and half-submerged near the top of the water were baby arrowhead leaves trying to take sprout against the odds of their position and circumstance. For days or weeks it would seem like the plant was suspended in time, and I would tell myself that I was doing right by it. But then one day, I'd notice the color on one of the leaves had changed again, and it would make me inexplicably and undeniably sad. The change in color was like an indicator of death, because death *is* change. And like life, it isn't still. We grow toward, through, in, and after death. We grow *because* of death.

That plant cannot continue to survive in that bottle, I'd admit, silently to myself. Without soil, its roots lacked necessary nourishment. The leaves might continue to recognize the sun, but as time passed they would also continue to fade. Green would become yellow, and then tan and then brown and then dry up like a scar—and then what story would I tell myself about it?

Never mind, I'd say, shaking away any next thought. When the water in the St-Germain bottle got too foggy, I'd carefully pour it all out and fill it up fresh—making sure not to run the tap so hard that it bruised the roots. Flourishing despite its imminent death, the plant reminded me of my father. But I could not seem to bring myself to put the plant in soil, because in so many ways: the plant also reminded me of *myself*.

By my midthirties, I had dumped myself out and started

fresh countless times. Following college I landed a really good job as a child protection social worker, but after two years I could not wait to get out of there. I left for the Peace Corps, in part because Peace Corps service is—inherently—temporary. I spent twenty-seven months of my life living in the freedom and fluidity that a new country can bring, and then I moved on. When I was watering the plants in the St-Germain center-piece bottle, I had just recently become a yoga teacher. I didn't know it yet, but I would—eventually—leave that job too. I was renting an attic bedroom, filling my home with hand-me-downs from my neighborhood Buy Nothing group, and living with a rotating cast of roommates.

Allowing myself to outgrow my container was what had brought me thus far, and part of me feared that laying down roots would rob me of my ability to keep growing, keep living, keep turning the page and finding my next chapter. I was afraid to allow my life to become still. I told myself that stability required too much digging, and it wasn't safe to just trust that an available soil would provide me with the nourishment I needed to take root. And yet: I have always been attracted to permanence. I want relationships fertilized to endure. I want love that lasts forever.

But the problem with permanence is that, for me, so often it begins to feel like being stuck. Stuck in Wisconsin, stuck in relationships that make me miserable, stuck in jobs I've grown out of. Stuck in feelings I didn't want to feel anymore. The basic expectations of everyday adulting: i.e., waking up and going through the motions of life—day after day—generally exhaust me until I feel slowly, suddenly, and inevitably numb. To combat my numbness, I will—eventually—start looking for a way to break the glass. Stretch out, sprout new life. At the time (and in many ways still now) it seemed easier to do that if the ground underneath my feet was fluid and in my control.

So there I was: water rooting my centerpieces and pretending there was such a thing as a living still life. I wanted the vines in the St-Germain bottle to grow, and I wanted them to stay the same for forever. I wanted to surround them with the freedom and fluidity of water, and I wanted them to somehow take permanent root—despite the inadequate conditions I was providing.

Over time, this plant began to serve as a reminder that the beauty of any living thing is—ultimately—temporary, impermanent. I would walk past the vines in the St-Germain bottle, sigh, and think about how growth—including death—is a demonstration of impermanence, and therefore of beauty, and therefore of life.

So: Sometimes, my plants will die. Sometimes I wait until they droop—wait for them to threaten me with an impending death—before I water them. Sometimes I provide them with beautiful yet inevitably unsurvivable conditions, and sometimes I nourish them with the safe, permanent, and fertile soil I know they need to take root. Sometimes I watch their leaves sprout, and other times I watch them fade. When I am wise, I remind myself that all of this is simply the way life is lived. And often none of it—what happens with my plants or even what happens with me—has anything to do with whether or not I am doing anything right. My gifted houseplants and home filled with hand-me-downs lived a life before me, and I can never know all the details of their pasts. I find comfort in not knowing, in imagining their stories. There is comfort in attempting to tell that story, and there is comfort in never being able to tell it.

•   •   •

One day, without planning to, I removed the pothos from the St-Germain bottle and allowed the arrowhead to thrive. The leaves suddenly perked up, in the way "suddenly" happens to houseplants: slow motion and fast like breath fading in the air. And despite still being rooted in water, the arrowhead began to grow, its tip delicately reaching across my table.

As I put the pothos vines into the compost bin, I was reminded of the time Uncle Ato told me that I would never have become who I am if my father were still alive. My me-ness would have been impacted by his presence, and therefore my me-ness is dependent upon his absence. I am not grateful that he died any more than I wish he were still alive. My father's death, quite simply and endlessly complicatedly, is just part of my life. Part of my story.

I secured the lid to the compost bin, exhaled, and went on with my day. *It'll get turned into something else*, I reminded myself. *Its death will help another thing grow.*

And it did, every day, right in front of me: the pothos' absence allowed the arrowhead to endure. And then—in a story I am no longer privy to—it nourished a soil and did that as compost for something else.

MY MOTHER'S BASEMENT

When I signed the lease on the very first apartment I would rent all on my own, I knew the one piece of furniture I wanted to bring with me. It was my mom's rocking chair.

My mom remembers buying the rocking chair when she started working full-time. With the extra income, she and my dad found themselves with flex in their budget, so they could afford to make a splurge purchase. The rocking chair cost two hundred dollars, which was a lot of money back then (and now!), and it is a beautiful piece of furniture. Granted, I don't know anything about carpentry, but this thing was solid, dark, gorgeous wood—maybe oak. My favorite part of the rocking chair was the headrest, which looked like a stretched-out heart with florals embossed on it. All of the edges of the rocking chair were rounded, though in retrospect I don't know if they were sanded to be that way, or if they became that way over time—the way things become a bit rounder when you love them.

My mom didn't have the rocking chair when I was born, but there's a picture of me sitting in it at about five months of age. Of course I don't have any actual memories of being an infant, but as I grew up, I began to develop all of these idyllic ideas about my mom rocking us kids in this chair, nursing us in it. I imagined it was where she read us bedtime stories and soothed our sick baby bodies while giving us medicine. And, since I found my first apartment when I was just twenty-four years old (some time before I would witness my big sister's nipple turn into what I can only describe as something that resembled partially cooked hamburger meat as she failed to unlatch her newborn baby while attempting to breastfeed him), the idea of nursing or tending to a sick, crying infant still seemed like a really beautiful thing to me, like the kind of life I should want to cultivate for myself.

In the years leading up to my first apartment, the rocking chair lived in the basement of my mom's house. That distinction—my *mom's* house, as opposed to *our* house—is intentional here. Because one day, when I was still just a senior in high school, my mom and I were driving to *our* house in Mequon when—out of nowhere—she turned to me and said, *Oh hey, d'ya wanna go by my new house?*

Your new what?! I asked.

My new house, she replied casually and without reacting to the hype of my response. *It's not done yet, because it's a new build, but I like to go by and check in on the progress, ya'know.*

No, I did not know. In fact, this was the first I was hearing of my mom building a new house. It was the first I was hearing of my mom having any desire to live anywhere other than the home she had created for us. I just kinda sat there—stunned. How could she have made this decision without me?

As we drove toward the build site, not far from the late-night Taco Bell on the corner of 91st and Good Hope that my friends and I liked to drive-thru on our way home from house parties in the city, my mom told me that my siblings all already knew about her new house. She just kept using those words: "my new house." Her phrasing felt deliberate, and each time those three little syllables hit me like a tiny knife.

My mom's new house would have three bedrooms—one for her and one for each of my younger siblings. Two years prior to its build, my big sis had graduated from high school, enrolled in college in Minnesota, and made it clear she wouldn't be moving back to Wisconsin. As my mom's new walls were being erected, I was preparing for my own high school graduation and registering for college in Green Bay. My little sis would graduate two years behind me, and our little brother a handful of years behind that. I guess it's normal for a parent to transform a college kid's bedroom into a gym, office, or crafting space—but my mother building an entire house while omitting any intentional space for me to live in it with her felt like a step beyond empty-nesting behavior. Without a room of my own in my mother's new home, I felt like she was saying that she didn't need me anymore.

A few months after seeing the skeleton of my mom's new house for the first time, I left for college and took only what would fit into my shared, 260-square-foot dorm room. About a month into my freshman year, I drove the hour from Green Bay to Mequon and found my adolescent home was a maze of brown cardboard moving boxes. I gathered a few empty ones, went up the stairs, and haphazardly threw everything from my purple, blue, and green bedroom into them. I lined one of my dad's old vintage suitcases with my CD collection, and considered taking my twin-size, dELiA*s-catalog rainbow-striped comforter and butterfly-print bedsheets with me, but my dorm room bed was an XL twin. I'd officially outgrown those adolescent bedclothes, so I tossed them into a box in the hallway with the rest of my mom's linens and left. I didn't need them anymore.

A few weeks later, I spent my first Thanksgiving break in my mom's new home—a house I was entering for the first time ever. I had to print out a MapQuest to get there, and when I warmed up my turkey leftovers, I didn't know which drawer to look in for forks. I slept on a futon my mom had purchased for her new sunroom, next to the family computer and our pet bird, and I spent the entire weekend bitching about how I didn't have a home anymore.

Little bits of that adolescent angst still come rushing through my veins when I tell the story of my mom's new house, but these days I am also filled with a gentle compassion for her. My mom left home just before graduating high school, but her move from Ghana to Wisconsin was a lot bigger than my transition from Mequon to Green Bay. Plus, in the years before that, *her* mom had left.

My grandfather was somewhat notoriously unfaithful, and while I respect my grandmother's decision to leave, I can only imagine the wound my mom must have felt from being left behind. But my mom never had the kind of life that allowed her the space to dwell on her emotions. My grandmother's leaving forced my mom, the oldest of her school-age siblings, to grow up quickly and take care of the little ones in the house. Years later when my mom arrived at her first American home, the plan was just as much for her to complete high school and go to college as it was to be a nanny for my uncle Ato's children. In his home, my mom slept on a small bed in a shared room with her niece, who was now in her charge.

As you well know by now, nearly two decades later my parents would purchase their first home—the split-level in River Falls—and my mom's life would afford her mere years of living the dream she'd been cultivating for herself, before her life partner would die. With four children crowding any space she might otherwise have had for her own emotions, my mother would move her family across the state to a suburban school district that often ranked among the best in Wisconsin. After a near decade of paying into that system, my mom was now cashing out. She was determined to enroll my brother in the 220 program and move to this new house in the city where she actually wanted to be.

As a college freshman, I had a glorified "bootstraps" perception of my mother's lived experience. I had no clue that in her freshman year of college, my mom often lacked a sense of belonging in her newfound home of Wisconsin. White folks were generally uninterested in befriending Black folks, and the other Black girls at Marquette University didn't want to be her friend either. Scooting away from her if she tried to sit next to them in class or at the cafeteria, they would hold their noses and say she smelled like Africa.

As a college freshman struggling to make new friends or figure out where I was welcomed to sit in the dining hall, I could only think about myself and my own life—so it didn't occur to me that my mother might have empathy for what I was experiencing. It didn't occur to me that the time I spent telling her how awful of a parenting decision she'd made in creating a home that didn't feel like it included me would have been time better spent trying to understand her lived history that might have led her toward those decisions. It didn't occur to me that slowing down and listening up to my mom's story would have made me feel less alone—and perhaps less abandoned.

Homesick for anything familiar and constant, I reacted instead with outrage. And true to her form, my mother eventually relented. By summer vacation she had created a post-construction bedroom in the basement for Veronica and me. And as we cleared out a space for the new bedroom, I began to affectionately refer to its surroundings as "The Thrift Store Called My Mother's Basement."

It seemed like this woman was holding on to every piece of furniture we had ever owned. Every coffee table, every end table, every lamp, every mattress, every bed frame, every *everything* we had *ever* owned was just a maze of stuff surrounding my makeshift bedroom. In my head, *I* was doing the work of putting my past into storage—like all of those neatly arranged suitcase CDs. But my mom? Well: *Honestly*, I thought, *this woman is just being a bit lazy.* Clearly, *she's* not doing the work of getting rid of things she'd moved on from.

Five years later, when I was faced with furnishing my first solo apartment at age twenty-four—it finally occurred to me that maybe my mom had been doing it for us. Maybe she was holding on to these piles of furniture so that her four children might have it a bit easier when we began to build homes for ourselves. And so, taking advantage of the wealth of free furniture in The Thrift Store Called My Mother's Basement, I asked my mom to bring the rocking chair when she helped me move into my new apartment. Dutifully and without question, my mother lugged its awkward frame up the stairs of her house and drove it the hour north to me in Green Bay.

My new apartment would become furnished with quite a few items from my mom's basement: the rocking chair, a full-size mattress, the corresponding bed frame. But it would also include several things I purchased for myself: like a really beautiful purple couch and love seat set with a funky, swirly pattern and chubby, chrome, rounded legs. The set was my first real, adult purchase. With a move pending and zero extra flex in my budget, I'd admired and paid for the set over several months as it sat in the display window of a furniture store in downtown Green Bay, before finally making it mine. My new apartment felt the same way: at long last, mine. I'd gone from living on campus for four years to splitting a four-bedroom house between five roommates, a dog, and a pet rabbit to finally living on my own. It seemed only fitting that the rocking chair I loved so much would be part of the life I was beginning to build for myself.

But I ended up living in that apartment for only about a year. When I left it was to join the Peace Corps, so I couldn't take my Willy Wonka couch, the rocking chair, the full-size mattress— or anything other than what could fit into two suitcases—with me. Once again I took advantage of my mother's basement and stored the entire contents of my apartment in my basement bedroom (which, unsurprisingly, I hadn't slept in since the summer after my junior year in college, once I realized it was silly to sleep all the way down in the basement when I could be closer to my mom and the rest of the family if I just crashed on the futon). My mom bought giant sheets of sticky plastic furniture covers, we wrapped the couch and love seat, and I left.

When I returned from the Peace Corps, my resettlement allowance afforded me some flex in my budget, so I splurged on a brand-new queen-size mattress for my next apartment in Chicago. I brought along the rocking chair, the Willy Wonka living room set, and a few other furnishings I'd started to accumulate along the way. Then, after just a year in Chicago, I was on the move again: this time toward Boston—strapping my queen-size mattress to the top of my mom's mini-SUV. We tried, but the rocking chair did not make the cut. Its awkward shape was too complicated for the Tetris game we created in the two cars that drove me across the country.

My decision to leave the rocking chair behind seemed inconsequential at the time. My mom was still hanging on to all of the old lamps, couches, and coffee tables, so why would the rocking chair be any different? Never once did I think I needed to actually communicate my nostalgia for the chair to my mother, nor did I think I needed to tell her that I wanted her to hold on to the rocking chair for me. Frankly: I hadn't been raised to communicate very well, if at all.

When my dad died, we took his pictures off the wall, stopped telling his stories, and we tried to find a way to rebuild a life without him. In those early years in Boston, my relatively nascent (and likely trauma-damaged) prefrontal cortex was beginning to solidify an adult ability to regulate and express my thoughts and emotions, and yet part of me still figured that since it didn't appear anyone really cared about much of anything scattered down in my mom's basement: there was no real reason to to ask for what I wanted.

I was wrong, though, because about a year into my living in Boston, my mom got rid of the rocking chair. She mentioned it in passing when we were chatting on the phone one night—like it was no big deal. One of her medical assistants was pregnant, and my mom gave her the rocking chair as a baby shower gift. Phone in my hand and mouth agape, I just kind of sat there—stunned. And then—true to form—I was outraged.

Mom! I screamed. *Don't you know that I associate that rocking chair with my childhood?! I had dreams of nursing my chil-*

dren in that chair, I told her. I was gonna read them bedtime stories and soothe their sick baby bodies in it just like she had for us. Although, as I've said, I didn't have any actual memories of her having ever done that. At the time, I didn't even know why my parents had bought the rocking chair, nor did I know why my mom had held on to it for all those years. In fact, I didn't know much of anything about any decisions my mom had ever made, because I'd never asked.

My relationship with my mother had always been one of her giving things to me—creating and providing things for me—and me receiving the fruits of her labor. There was little to no expectation that I do anything to actively retrieve from the bounty my mom had spent a lifetime cultivating for us, her now adult children. I didn't articulate my needs, or my gratitude when they'd been fulfilled, and she wasn't going to ask for recognition either.

At the time, I was working as a youth services social worker, and I had come to hate—and love—the experience of being someone's grown-up (or in my mom's case: someone's parent). What made me most uncomfortable was the fact that you just never know when you were doing something they'd never forget. You never know which observation of you processing your own emotions will become the manual for how they express theirs. You never know which of the things you give them will become the things they held on to forever, nor which of your words will grow into a life lesson. So there I was, sobbing about an old piece of furniture to my mom across a cell phone connection of a thousand miles. And her response became a lesson I will never forget.

You know, Theresa, she said calmly and without reacting to the hype of my response. *I'm not responsible for holding on to the things that matter to you.*

This time my mother's words were not a tiny knife. They were a ton of bricks. And it would be nice if I could say that I took those bricks and swiftly built something with them. I wish I could tell you I immediately integrated her message into a more adult, mature understanding of the requirement for me to name, claim, and articulate what I need or want from the people who love me. But it didn't happen like that.

I'm told that readers seek a "bathroom floor moment"— the main character curled up in the fetal position, a montage of her historical missteps playing before her eyes. The narrator would eloquently describe the memory of her cheek against the cool tile floor, and after she'd exhausted herself from mournful, private sobs, our heroine would fall asleep in a puddle of her tears surrounded by damp wads of tissue, before emerging like a phoenix from the ashes: a brand-new warmth and sense of self in her heart.

And you know what? I get it. That sounds really beautiful, but I don't have that scene to give you. I am neither an always-insightful character nor a perfect narrator, and just as my mother's life has rarely afforded her the space to dwell in her emotions, mine did not naturally afford me the tools to feel or even readily recognize my own. My tears have rarely flowed in moments of private, rock-bottom sorrow. They've instead poured out of me like daggers aimed at those I love most—not infrequently: my mother. No matter what I was trying to cultivate in my life—anger, angst, and garden-variety bitching had become my go-to response for almost any degree of discomfort. My most easily accessible, lowest-hanging fruit.

Plenty of experiences require that rock-bottom for change to happen, but even more just require an empty tank, eventually refueled with something better for the system to operate. So while I know it didn't happen in some coming-of-age, rom-com-esque bathroom floor scene, I don't know when—

exactly—I stopped being a person who was only able to reach for her lowest-hanging fruit. What I know is that finding her took time, and that I did—eventually—become her. As I sobbed about the rocking chair on the phone with my mom that day, perhaps my fuel gauge light illuminated itself. But this wouldn't be the first, nor the last, time that I would drive around on a near-empty tank.

Eventually, I would also become a person who asks my mom about her life, a person who wants to understand my mother as a human being with motivations that are sometimes about building a life for her children and anticipating their needs, but other times are solely focused on creating the life she desires for herself. So—since I've become an adult who asks—I can tell you that my mom does not remember that phone call at all. She knows she gave the rocking chair away as a baby shower gift, she vaguely recalls that I was upset about it, but for her: this was just another phone call. And truthfully, even *I* didn't know in the moment that this phone call would become one of my permanent, core memories.

And *that* is what it's really like to be someone's grown-up. There are some seeds that you plant on purpose. You hold them in the palm of your hand, transfer them to your fingertips, place them directly into the earth, and wait to see them flower and fruit. And then there are things that grow by accident. Imagine a field filled with dandelion puffs, and a child playfully running through that field, spreading the seeds with each stomp of their foot. Then imagine that some of those seeds get stuck on that kid's clothing, and just drop throughout the rest of that child's life—without you or the child even realizing that it's happening. *That* is what being someone's grown-up feels like for me. It's a responsibility far too terribly overwhelming for me to bear.

When my mom gave away the rocking chair, I still believed that I was cultivating a life for my eventual children, because I was still telling myself that I wanted children. I have since arrived at a realization to the contrary, an admission that parenthood is not a thing I ever actually wanted for myself. I love working with youth and witnessing them figuring themselves out, but when I finally took the time to ask myself what I wanted, I would recognize that the lifelong commitment of parenthood isn't one I have any interest in making. To be honest, it's a decision I don't even fully understand. Just as I ask couples how they met because I do not understand the rules one follows to get you there, I also do not understand the rules one follows—or even the true motivation behind—someone voluntarily deciding to raise children.

One morning when I was in my early thirties and had just completed a day of preparing Thanksgiving dinner for my younger siblings, their partners, and my mom—I woke up and realized that I needed to make everyone breakfast. Throughout every day of their visit, the kitchen and bathroom garbage got full before sunset, while the cupboards became conversely empty. I'd slept that night on a blow-up mattress on the floor of my bedroom in Boston, relinquishing my queen-size bed to my mother.

Mom? I asked in the early morning light. *Are you awake?*

Yea, she replied groggily, *I'm awake.*

Mom, why did you do this? Why did you have all these kids, all these mouths to feed?

What I wanted to know—what I was trying to ask—was why were *we* the responsibility *she* chose to bear? And I wondered if she had ever taken the time to ask herself the question.

I don't know, my mom replied. *It's just the life I always wanted.*

By then my mother no longer had a basement. After about a decade of living in her new house, she was forced to admit she would have to sell it (since, in my opinion, she—like many buyers at the turn of the millennium—had been sold lies about what they could afford). One by one, my mom called each of her adult children to tell us she was losing her home. It was maybe the first time she had openly and collectively informed us of a major life decision before it happened, but she didn't tell us because we asked. She didn't tell us because she wanted to, or even because she chose to. She told us because she had to. She needed us.

When my mom said goodbye to her home, I had zero expectation that she would do the work of clearing out her basement. The past that lived down there was not hers alone to let go of. Instead, my siblings and I split the cost of a dumpster and scheduled a rotation of times when we would make our way home to help Mom pack up her life. We salvaged what could go to Goodwill (like all of my old CDs and the vintage suitcase), we rescued what we wanted (our family photo albums came with me to Boston, Dad's old desk made its way to Veronica's home in Minnesota, the formal dining table and chairs went to Affi's house in Milwaukee, and my brother held on to some of Dad's old vinyls and one of his old blazers), and we tossed the rest.

My mom held on to the things that mattered to her, signed a rental lease on a town house, and moved on. My mom's new town house was the first home she would create for herself, without any of her children. She brought along her kitchen table, her dresser, her bed, and the museum-print image of a tiny insect on a single blade of grass that had hung above my parents' bed since before my dad died (*He used to love that picture*, she's told me). On my first visit to the town house, I didn't know where to find the forks—and yet this place immediately felt like home to me. I thought I had taken all of our family photo albums to Boston, but as I walked around the town house I learned that I was wrong. Separate from the ones stored in her former basement, my mom had long held on to the photos that felt closest to her heart—and so this town house became the first home where my mom finally hung photos of my father back up on the wall. One of the guest bedrooms held my old daybed, and I slept on the futon in the other guest space, surrounded by photos of my father, my mom's mom, my dad's mom, myself, my siblings, their children. And when I opened the linen closet, I found my mom had carefully folded and preserved my decades-old, twin-size dELiA*s bedsheets.

This was the first time since before I was in elementary

school that my mom did not own her home. And in that transition, she lost a piece of the life she had always wanted. Lost part of the life she'd been cultivating, and put to rest (for now at least) the dream of homeownership she and my dad had shared and first achieved together. Although honestly, in many ways, that dream likely died with him.

. . .

More than ten years after my mom lost her home, I realized I wanted to buy a home of my own. And like many of my most important decisions, this one didn't happen in a single scene. I had been renting since just after college—when I shared that space with my four roommates, a dog, and a rabbit—and had been attempting to build a home for myself since that first solo apartment with my Willy Wonka couch set and the rocking chair. I'd paid and lost more security deposit dollars than I care to calculate, allowing one landlord after another to financially penalize the basic wear and tear, rounded-out edges of my life, by calling it damage. In the last apartment I would rent, my landlord told me upon my moving in that the gauge on the tank of oil providing heat and hot water to my unit was broken. *I'll keep an eye on it*, he promised me, *and I'll make sure they refill it before it ever goes empty.* Instead, he routinely let me go for days without heat or hot water, making me feel passively chastised for using more oil than any of his previous tenants, and then sent me a massive back-pay bill when he realized he'd forgotten to charge me for any of the refills. This, I told myself, would be the last time I would run on an empty tank.

Homeownership had never been a life goal of mine, but once it became one: I was fully committed to achieving it. After a year of searching, two teams of Realtors, and six rejections: I finally had an offer accepted in July of 2022. Sixty days later—at the age of thirty-nine—I became the first of my mother's children to independently find, purchase, and own a home (well, okay, the bank owns it—the bank owns a lot of houses, but they call *me* a homeowner now). When I moved into my condo, I brought with me the things that matter to me, not just because I paid for them, but because I have—on purpose—held on to them.

On the promise that they'll never have to contribute to me having a baby shower, I invited my friends and family to Venmo me so I could furnish and decorate my new home. During the pandemic, my mom had sent me those dELiA*s butterfly bedsheets to make into Covid masks—a relic of my past life re-created into something new—and I wore them whenever the paint, wallpaper glue, or cleaning chemical fumes involved in making the condo my home became too overwhelming. Much like the bedroom I haphazardly moved out of in Mequon, I painted the walls of this home in (more mature tones of) purple, green, and blue. I hung Marimekko wallpaper in the living room, and bought a two-hundred-dollar simplehuman brand garbage can for the kitchen (hey, flex in the budget = can afford to splurge, right?).

This is not the first home I have built for myself, but in many ways it feels like the first time I have truly been able to *create* a home for myself. These walls, this floor, the bathroom ceiling that I painted Benjamin Moore's Sharp Cheddar gold, and everything within this space all belong to me now. This is the first time I can ask myself what I want my home to be like, and then fully articulate my response in every corner of the place. Every decision I make about my home is entirely for me.

But I would be lying if I told you I don't have to sometimes talk myself into keeping up on the work of creating and maintaining this home. Without children, I'm just growing this garden for me. I have to remind myself to believe that the flowers blooming here matter, even when sometimes I'm the only one who smells them. No one is going to cry when I eventually get rid of my Nigerian-print couch, because no one but me is fantasizing a future for it. There is no lasting consequence to the decisions I make over which pieces of my life are the ones I want to hold on to forever, because my forever will die with me.

As I grow this life in my new home, my mom's lesson about her decision to get rid of the rocking chair continues to bear fruit. It's up to me to realize what I want for myself, up to me to ask, and up to me to respond. I am responsible for living the life I want to live, and for living it on and with purpose. So was, and is, my mom.

Sure, The Thrift Store Called My Mother's Basement was filled with relics of the life she was once trying to build. It was filled with things she hoped would help furnish the lives of her children. But it was also filled with things that she just wanted to hold on to, entirely and only for herself. Because really, what's a basement if not an underground space filled with seeds that will—eventually—impact the life growing up above it.

BLACKITY-BLACK

When Megan Thee Stallion hosted *Saturday Night Live* in 2022, her opening monologue included the phrase "hoodrat stuff with my hoodrat friends," and also spoke to Megan completing her bachelor's degree. I almost cried when she performed "Anxiety"—my favorite song from her latest album—and her closing skit had a joke about the concept of duality. At the time, I was working through revisions of this essay collection and had just workshopped an earlier version of "White Kids." The workshop readers asked how some of the essay characters are doing now (*Oh, you know . . . Midwest, married, two kids and a dog*). And one said that while it was clear that the narrator (i.e., current-Theresa) got out, it was not yet clear *how*.

I posted about Megan's *SNL* performance on Facebook, and my best friend from high school commented, *Can't even imagine what it was like for you to grow up as we did. I think about it a lot.* Her comment made me feel at the same time deeply seen while deeply reflective and thankful that I no longer feel the need to constantly prove myself. I have precious few things in common with Megan Thee Stallion—including where and how we grew up—but somehow her duality feels akin to mine. Somehow, watching Megan Thee Stallion on *Saturday Night Live* reminded me of witnessing myself trying to compose this book.

. . .

In my sophomore year at Homestead High School, the other Black girls in my grade started a club called Sisters of Nzinga, named for an Angolan queen who is honored and remembered as a protector of her people. I was the only Black girl in my grade whose parents were African immigrants, and the only Black girl in my grade not invited to join the club.

I was, silently, devastated.

But I never had any means for responding to this devastation. Sisters of Nzinga was one of many reminders that no matter how much I tried to be like the other Black girls at school, I would fail because if I wanted to be in any way true to myself: I would never be enough for what they seemed to expect of me. If high-school-me told my mom about Sisters of Nzinga (as I'm sure I did) the only response I can imagine her having was that I didn't need a club to connect me to Africa. I had her. I had Uncle Ato, who sometimes gave us Fante language lessons on Saturday mornings so that we would understand even better who we were and where we came from. And even though he was dead, I had my dad. We are Black. *We* are African.

After my experience with Sisters of Nzinga, it did not occur to me that any of the Black girls at my college would want to be friends with me. There were a handful of other Black students at UW–Green Bay, most originating—of course—from Milwaukee, and I was completely blind to any attempts they made at befriending me. In my first month on campus, another Black freshman named Raegan walked past me in the hall and waved. I responded as though her tongue were about to lash out at me with the mockery I'd come to expect from my childhood playgrounds—diverting my eyes and speeding away in the other direction.

When my mom tells me about meeting my dad, she says that despite how generally shy she is, she was never nervous to exchange smiles with him at that library at Marquette. *We are both African*, she says, *and Africans say hello to each other*. Similarly, when Raegan tried to wave at me in the hall that day: she was just one Black girl saying, *Hey girl*, to another Black girl. Luckily, she kept trying, and I got better at noticing.

Raegan would become one of my first Black friends who never made fun of me for who I was, and never expected me to be anyone or anything other than who I am. Sure, she thought it was a bit odd that before the Black Student Union's Soul Food Dinner my freshman year, I'd never eaten collard greens. But she learned how to pronounce my Nigerian middle name, and she was the first friend to ever call me Ini. Raegan listened to 112, Maroon 5, and Jagged Edge, and I would drive to Green Bay's branch of The Exclusive Company CD store to buy the new Ani, Sleater-Kinney, or Jurassic 5 as soon as they were released. This mismatch in our musical tastes wasn't a problem—not for her, and not for me. It no longer mattered to me if I had everything in common with my friends, and more importantly: I was—less and less—seeking external validation for my Blackness.

But: even Raegan recently asked me when I got to be "so Black, like Blackity-Black."

It wasn't a question I could answer, because identity doesn't have a when. It doesn't subscribe to a timeline. It didn't happen all at once. Rather, I've spent my adult life inching toward my identity. A self-defined, internally validated version of me.

•   •   •

At some point in 2018, my siblings and I decided to get a sibling tattoo. We spent months texting ideas back and forth. Among the vetoed suggestions were a Totoro (one of our favorite childhood movies), a slice of mushroom pizza (Veronica's favorite topping), and a Sankofa (Affi already had one on her shoulder). Sitting around the kitchen table at my mom's town house one night, we finally agreed on a paintbrush.

In the backyard of our split-level home in River Falls, we had a birch tree. We called it "the paper tree" because its white bark—the first we had ever seen—peeled off like sheets of paper. It was the only tree of its kind in the yard. And using a big bucket of muddy water and house-painting brushes from our dad's toolbox, we would paint the tree brown.

Don't you guys think it's kinda weird how we used to do that?

I asked as I sketched a paintbrush for our tattoo. *Like, we painted the* one *white tree in the yard* brown. . . . *What do you think that meant? Don't you think it* meant *something . . . ?*

My little sister rolled her eyes and quickly retorted, *No, Theresa. It doesn't* mean *anything. Not everything has to* mean *something. This isn't one of your stories. Just draw the tattoo!* (Which admittedly: was a fair response. Sorry not sorry for being the writer in the family ::hard shrug::.)

As I passed around the paintbrush sketch—a rounded-off handle with a row of teeth spanning about three times the width of the handle itself—someone remarked how it looked like a hair pick. And just like that, we arrived at a unanimous decision. Our dad's hair pick.

It was a black, hard plastic comb with a Black Power fist embossed on the end of the handle. Certainly, my siblings and I each have a different relationship with the hair pick, and with the Black Power fist in general. For me, what has always stood out about the fist is the way the thumb wraps around the other fingers. And, if you'll indulge me to alter this visual a bit, that reminds me of how my dad's memory wraps him around the five of us: me, my mom, my siblings. I often think of "my family" as a party of five, but really we are six.

It took another year or so for my siblings and me to finally get our tattoos. My little bro didn't quite want to follow suit with his sisters, so he opted instead for two symbols—one from Ghana and one from Nigeria—to be tatted on his knuckles. My sisters and I each got a carbon copy of the hair pick: Affi's on her hip, Veronica's on her forearm, and mine on my chest. We decided to add a swoop to the comb, like a parenthesis lying on its side, borrowed from the Ghanaian Duafe symbol for beauty.

My sibling tattoo was my seventh, and its healing process was incredibly challenging. Like any fresh ink, this one was perfect on day one. It was surprisingly unpainful to receive, the lines were crisp, and the photo of me admiring it in the mirror in the tattoo shop is one of my favorite images of myself. Placed directly above my heart and therefore conveniently covered by everyday clothing, this tattoo, however, began to bleed and puff and peel and scab more than any tattoo I've ever had before or since. In the weeks that followed I would catch myself eyeing it in the bathroom mirror—I was, silently, devastated—and tinged with an uncomfortable feeling, akin to shame, or embarrassment.

I have spent my life wanting to feel like I was part of something. A member of the club. When I made that post about Megan Thee Stallion on my Facebook, I copy pasted the text to my Black People Who Watch TV group, a community I joined because while it's nice to be seen by my White friends from high school for how much of an outsider I was during that time in my life, it is even nicer to talk about that with people who might have a shared experience. I am a member of the Black Girls Who Love Fur Babies group and the Boston Writers of Color group and a cofounder of the Boston BIPoC Yogis—but all of these clubs, all of these groups, are only on Facebook. And is Facebook even real? Is my belonging real? Do I really belong to and with anyone?

I don't like to admit it, but part of me knows that when I got my sibling tattoo, I was—in part—efforting to brand myself with my Blackness. It is permanent ink, in my melanin, and now that it's there, no one can deny me of it. I don't like to admit that I felt this way, because what I'd rather feel is over it. Self-defined. Self-knowing. Non-seeking. I want to be the person who my mother and father and Uncle Ato raised me to be. I want to be the person I believe myself to be, the person I tell myself I am.

As I reclined in the tattoo chair that day, I imagine that part of my mind drifted to that oversize Looney Tunes T-shirt I bought back in the fifth grade. Was I doing that again? Adorning myself with a mere caricature of Blackness and hoping that everyone would interpret it as identity? Was *I* interpreting it as identity?

I know that not everything is one of my stories, but this is. So when I think of the healing process for my sibling tattoo— the way it peeled and scabbed and bled. When I look at it in the mirror today, its lines less sharp, the negative space blurred: It feels like a metaphor placed on my heart. I know what the tattoo is, but if I'm honest—I cannot be sure that anyone on the outside looking in at me would. And sometimes I'll look at my reflection in the mirror and tell myself, *It's better this way.* Better that what I was efforting to do, failed. Better that every time my chest is bare, I am reminded that the only interpretation of me that matters is my own. I need only define myself to and for myself.

So I cannot tell you, or Raegan, or anyone when or how I became so "Blackity-Black." And I don't owe that to you, to Raegan, or to anyone other than myself. What I will say is that this is who I've always been; it just took me awhile to communicate it. Took me awhile to know it. Took me awhile to realize that I don't need to be a member of any club to prove it.

I like to believe that this version of who I am is permanent, like a tattoo. And for the most part, I know it is *because* I know it's who I always was. But after more than four years of working on this essay collection, the one thing I have learned for certain is that with time: all stories blur.

THE OKOKON FAMILY
ORCHESTRA

My mom loves to sing, though she doesn't have what would conventionally be referred to as a "good" voice. Her standard range stays a solid two octaves above any song she sings, like if you can imagine Mariah belting out every note at her highest register but without it really sounding very nice? That's my mom. Even when she hums, it's high-pitched.

I like to believe that I inherited my love of singing (and my bad voice) from my mother. I often find myself absent-mindedly humming in a near falsetto down the aisle of some convenience store. And one of my favorite adult-child memories is sipping after-dinner drinks with my mom as we sing Bill Withers on the couch following a holiday meal.

My mom also loves musicals, and my sisters and I have come to love them as well. Our elementary school in River Falls put on a musical every year, and my mom would buy the movie version of that year's musical on VHS for us to watch over and over again at home. One year the school musical was *Bye Bye Birdie*, and my little sister got a minor role in the production, playing a sandwich-board smiley-face who mistakenly belted out her lyrics as *loopty-loo, and laugh at the view!* Another year, all the kids at school learned how to roll fake cigarette packs into our T-shirt sleeves for the production of *Grease*. And one year, my third-grade teacher, Ms. Moriarity—who would later coordinate stacks of sympathy cards for me and my family— played Miss Hannigan in *Annie*.

My mom used to keep cassette tapes in the glove compartment of our sky-blue Toyota Previa minivan, which we called "the Mongo-Moose," and she'd pop one in to keep us kids occupied on long rides. On short trips, whoever was up front controlled the soundtrack, but on longer rides that rule went out the window: so crowd-favorite cassette tapes were the best bet. One cassette in the Mongo-Moose's heavy rotation was the Canadian-cast rendition of *Joseph and the Amazing Technicolor Dreamcoat*, starring Donny Osmond.

The musical, written by Andrew Lloyd Webber and Tim Rice, is a direct translation of a short story in the book of Genesis. It's a tale of familial conflict and joyful resolution, and it happens to be one of my mom's favorite biblical stories. She's told me she still remembers learning about Joseph and his brothers in Sunday school as a young girl in Ghana. The Canadian cast of *Joseph and the Amazing Technicolor Dreamcoat* made a handful of stops in the Midwest during their international tour in the fall of 1992, and—a few months after my dad's death—my mom purchased tickets for our family.

Looking back, accepting that my dad had died and there was no further explanation as to how or why it happened was sort of like believing that a prisoner could become the Pharaoh's right-hand man. But us kids accepted it the same way centuries of believers have accepted stories bound in books or sung on stages. Some people get to become who they always wanted to be, and some don't. Some things you see are a dream, and some are real. Sometimes life makes sense; sometimes it doesn't. And sometimes, people just die.

As a kid, the story my mom told us about my dad's death was plain and not detailed. We learned not to ask how or why it happened, because somehow, we learned that there wasn't a clear answer to those simple yet incredibly complicated questions. He wasn't sick. He wasn't old. He didn't have an accident. But he was dead, and that was the end of the story.

My actual memory of seeing *Joseph* with my family that fall is, like much of the detail from the months immediately following my father's death, a blurry, gray fog. Instead, what stands out in full color is the way my brother began refusing to eat anything but breakfast foods, because to this day the smell of artificial maple syrup or cheese melting on eggs in the microwave still makes me nauseous. I remember the stack of handmade construction-paper cards from Ms. Moriarity and my classmates, and I remember how cared for those cards made me feel. I was the first of my siblings who wanted to go back to school, and I remember slowly realizing that all the kids were being nice to me at recess because they'd been told to.

My classroom participated in something called the Communications Unit, where a third-, fourth-, fifth-, and blended-grade special-education classroom all gathered on Friday mornings to sing songs accompanied by a teacher playing the acoustic guitar. Woody Guthrie's "This Land Is Your Land" and "I Want to Hold Your Hand" by the Beatles. It had been my favorite part of the week, but when I returned to school, I could hardly make it through a sing-along without crying. We would get a few chords into Diana Ross's "If We Hold On Together" from the soundtrack of *The Land Before Time*, and I would be weeping. I'm certain my dad didn't know a single word to that song, but the lyrics "I know our dreams will never die" were more than my little nine-year-old heart could handle.

Without a script of how to respond, no one at school quite knew what to do with me. A guidance counselor called me into her office, and after what was likely a tooth-pulling hour of trying to get me to talk about something for which I had no words to articulate, she sent me home with a book called *Daddy Doesn't Live Here Anymore*. I have to imagine she either hadn't realized it was a book about divorce or perhaps her library just didn't include a book for when a kid's parent dies. No one—my mother included—knew what to do or say. Instead, most people treated my family like a piece of glass that was about to shatter. Or maybe, in their eyes, we already had. Our shards precariously clinging together with glue, still wet like the tears on my third-grade cheeks.

But I never saw my mom cry. And while it's possible I went to her arms to be held while I cried, I don't remember that either. I, too, treated my mom like glass, and I didn't want to be the reason she fell apart at the seams she was trying so desperately to hold together. If there is a book that teaches you the "right" way to respond when the love of your life suddenly dies and you are left to raise your four children alone, it is not a book my mother had access to. Instead she let me go back to school when I wanted, she made my brother breakfast morning, noon, and night, and she took us to see *Joseph*.

I thought it would be fun, she tells me now.

My mom wouldn't have told us kids at the time, but it seems there were unprovable suspicions that my dad's family might have been involved in his death. So given that my mom knew the story of Joseph from having read it in Sunday school, it strikes me as a self-inflicted, painful choice to take her children to see a musical about an attempted familial murder. It makes me wonder if there was a moment—sitting in that theater surrounded by her children and a cacophony of colors, music, and lights—when that realization began to occur to my mother. A moment when the songs of Joseph's brothers plotting to kill him suddenly hit a little too close to home. It makes me wonder if she cried, silently, in that theater. And I wonder if she felt hopeful as the musical eventually reminded her of the story's happy ending. If she thought she, too, might somehow—miraculously—be able to manifest a happy ending for her own story. A family reunited. A moral. A meaning. A golden lining. Anything.

Once, sobbing with fear, I called my mom because I'd met a man I was certain I was meant to marry. After countless failed relationships, I was terrified I would lose this man, a fear I'm sure I inherited from both of my parents. My mom listened, reminded me to breathe, and between my gasps of air she said, *Oh, Theresa. I am so, so sorry. I wish I knew what to say. It's just, I have never felt what you are feeling. I have never felt this kind of fear; I never experienced the kind of sadness you are so afraid to feel again.*

I realized in that moment how different love must feel for my mom than it does for me. My mom got to feel a pure love, yet I have no real understanding of what that might be like. Her mind must have grayed out detail from the moments surrounding my dad's death, protecting her from the pain of constantly re-experiencing his loss, as much as my mind attempts to protect me. But I wonder what my mom remembers of that time. I wonder what her mind allowed her to feel through her heartbreak, what it allows her to feel of it now. I wonder what story she believes about his death, and what songs she sings when she wants to remember their love and the life they had together.

For me, music can be soothing, like water gently slipping across dried bits of blood on a wound. Other times, I can hear an old song and it dredges up tinges of pain in a place I thought was fully healed, and I'm suddenly choking back tears through my near-falsetto hums in the tampon aisle at Target. I've experienced more than my fair share of heartbreaks, but I cannot even begin to imagine an emotion that would compare to what my mom must have experienced when she lost her husband. So while I am filled with wonder, I do not ask my mom to pick at her scars any more than I willingly pick at my own. Instead, I seek out our mutual joy.

I saw a local production of *Joseph* recently, and texted a photo of the program to our family group chat after the show. My mom responded with a "So Jelly" Bitmoji, her cartoon avatar peeking out from a jar of purple sticky stuff. I called her to talk about the show, and after a short chat, she hung up and went to read her Bible. Then she called me back to recount the story as it happens in the book, and I reminded her of each part's corresponding song from the musical. When we got to the end—where Joseph has forgiven his brothers and is being reunited with his father—I sang, two octaves too high, *Give me my colored coat, my amazing colored coat!*

Ohhhh, my mom sighed, and I could hear her smile. *Oh, I love* Joseph. *We listened to that tape so much, I don't even know whatever happened to it. It probably melted,* she said, and chuckled.

It's cliché, but the music from that soundtrack embraces me like a childhood hug from my mother, even if I cannot remember her arms around me at the time. My little sister plays the songs for her kids, and when my family gets together, someone will almost inevitably make a *Joseph* reference. On a recent Spotify Wrapped, Andrew Lloyd Webber ranked among my favorite artists, and I still know every word to *Joseph.* I listen to it when I'm happy, and I listen to it when I'm sad. I listen to it when I'm cleaning the house and just need some background noise, and I listen to it when I'm night driving and need something to sing along with so I'll stay awake. There are moments when I try to sing all of the parts at once, and others when I hold back, as though someone else in the Mongo-Moose will jump in.

Through the foggy haze of my experience of my father's death, *Joseph and the Amazing Technicolor Dreamcoat* stands out like the psychedelic, multicolored magic that it is. Much of what my mind is able to conjure from that time—the smell of eggs in the microwave, my classmates' responses, my treasured morning sing-alongs—reverberates like a minor-key chord in my heart, that haunted, echoey, hollow-yet-full kind of sound that feels like heartbreak and falling in love all at the same time. But with *Joseph*, we transformed our minivan into an orchestra, our voices creating a colorful spot of pure joy in the midst of our collective gray fog. And that is exactly what my mom hoped for when she took us to the theater that fall. A good memory. A happy ending.

I thought it would be fun.

EPILOGUE
GO BACK AND FETCH IT

S ankofa (pronounced sahn-COH-fah) is a Twi word and
Adinkra symbol from Ghana meaning "go back and fetch
it." It is traditionally depicted as a bird standing on its own two
feet. The feet and heart of the bird face forward, while the bird's
head is turned back, reaching its beak for an egg that is resting
on its back. The Sankofa openheartedly—yet blindly—moves
forward while carrying its origins in the same place from which
it will tell its story.

Sometimes, Sankofa is depicted as two sides of a loopy
heart, and if you take a look at the fences or gates in your
neighborhood, you are likely to find this version, because en-
slaved West Africans made the Sankofa a standard image in

American metalworking. While a fence is meant to separate one thing from another: Black from White, solitude from love, truth from falsehood—I like to imagine that these ironworkers were infusing barriers with this symbol of the inherently loopy connection of time.

For better or for worse: our past is both our present and our future.

The Sankofa[1] is the single most important concept in my approach to storytelling. As I continue to move forward, I will always carry my past with me.

---

1. Alongside my father

ACKNOWLEDGMENTS

I just turned forty-one. I didn't know it at the time, but back when I was thirty-six, I started writing this book. Or maybe I started when I was twenty-seven, when I first wrote and told the story of my name for a Massmouth slam at Club Passim in Cambridge, Massachusetts. Or maybe I started when I was born. I guess in some ways, I've always been writing this book (wow, what an annoying writer-ish thing to say, jeez Louise).

No matter how you slice it, writing this book is among the longest gigs I've ever had—and as much as I am grateful beyond words to be at the finish line—I've been dragging my feet on writing this one last bit. The reasons for that are many, and if you've made it this far with my story, you could probably guess those reasons for yourself. As is the case with almost anything I have ever written, I've found myself buried under the pressure of not knowing where to start. Worried I would do it wrong. Afraid I would forget someone—or something—and spend the rest of my life wanting to scream how much they mean to me from every rooftop I'll ever encounter. I'm confident that will happen, so please accept my preemptive apology here. You. You matter to me. I am grateful for how you supported this book, grateful you are in my life.

My first and deepest thanks belong to my mother, who inexplicably believed in this book from the very beginning, who encouraged me as a creative being since childhood, who loves me limitlessly, even when I've done nothing to deserve it. Thank you, Mommy. I love you too.

I'd like to thank my siblings, Veronica, Affi, and Africanus, for your trust, love, friendship, willingness, and never-ending group chat support. Thank you to my mentor, Grace Talusan: I do not even have words to describe what you mean to me. Thank you, Uncle Ato, Cousin Eman, and all of the Yarney family. Thank you, Dad.

Thank you to my memoir teacher, Alysia Abbott, who carried the credit of naming this book until the verrrry last minute (sorry!). Thank you to all of my besties: Allison Dahl, Raegan Jackson, Alli Lurie, Jannelle Codianni, Panther, Peter Freeman and Anthony Verdino, Amy Laird, Anri Wheeler, and Becky Pasterski. Thank you to GrubStreet and my writing, Essay Incubator, and Memoir Incubator community, especially Kat Read, Thu-Hằng Trần, Ani Gjika, Angie Chatman, Lauren Rheaume, Lorena Hernández Leonard, Neema Avashia, and Aimee Christian. Thank you to my Massmouth and *Stories from the Stage* storytelling community, especially Cheryl Hamilton, Patricia Alvarado Núñez, Michael Rossi, Sophia Garcia, and Norah Dooley (again, there are not enough words). Thank you, Ms. Moriarity and Emily, for your conversation and for remembering me. Thank you to all of my students, including those with the Mission Hill Women's Writers Group, GrubStreet, the Boston Public Library, and Brigham and Women's Writing in Color.

Thank you to Roslindale, especially my Buy Nothing Group (lol); Marissa Puntigam (for the bagels, for the photos, for the friendship); and my roommates, Allison and Rey, for letting me basically take over our entire house as I sought out a change in scenery with a new room to write in. Thank

you to the restaurants where this manuscript was drafted, especially Quincy's Idle Hour and Eastie's Cunard. Thank you
to Follow Your Art in Melrose, to Tin House, to VONA, to
HippoCamp, to Muse in the Marketplace, to the tiny house
Airbnb in Pembroke, to Elizabeth's perfect studio in Newbury-
port, and to Ginny DeLuca and her cozy JP home. Thank you
to everyone who contributed to the GoFundMe that allowed
me to take Grace's class. Thank you to all of the readers who
provided feedback on Zoom meetings with me. Thank you to
Kim McLarin for calling me out in the most important way.
Thank you to everyone who has believed that my writing de-
served to be out in the world, especially *midnight & indigo*,
Hippocampus Magazine, Brettne Bloom, and Michelle Herrera-
Mulligan. Thank you to my yoga practice and community.

Thank you to Facebook, Instagram, GoogleDrive, and
the Call Recorder app—although (not to be too Snoop Dogg
about it), I guess that is also just me thanking myself. Which,
I suppose, also belongs here too. So, thank you, self, for never
quitting on telling this story. Thank you to the writers (yet
to be named here) who have informed my writing: folks like
Kiese Laymon, Carmen Maria Machado, CJ Hauser, and Rox-
ane Gay (I'm all of y'alls biggest fangirl, let's be friends?).

And finally thank YOU, dear reader. Thank you for hearing me, thank you for listening to me, thank you for holding my narrative so carefully in your hands. And if you have a story of your own to tell: thank you in advance for telling it.

Because like my mom says: Someone should tell it.

❤ theresa

ABOUT THE AUTHOR

Theresa Okokon is a Pushcart Prize–nominated essayist. A Wisconsinite living in New England, she is a writer, a storyteller, and the cohost of *Stories from the Stage*. In addition to writing and performing her own stories, Theresa also teaches storytelling and writing workshops and classes, coaches other tellers, hosts story slams, and frequently emcees events for nonprofits. She is an alum of both the Memoir Incubator and Essay Incubator programs at GrubStreet.

Theresa's essays (and bathroom selfies!) have appeared in *midnight & indigo*, *Elle*, the *Independent*, WBUR's *Cognoscenti*, and on Boston.com. Her essay "Me Llamo Theresa," published by *Hippocampus Magazine* and nominated for a 2020 Pushcart Prize, was recognized among the "Top 5 Longreads of the Week" by Longreads and "This Week in Essays" by the Rumpus.

Theresa Instagrams gorgeous cocktails, food porn, and pics about Blackness, fatness, and her very cute senior dog at @ohh.jeezzz.